Gramma and Grandpa
Thank you for inspiring me.

Mom and Dad
Thank you for caring.

Acknowledgments

When I have read the acknowledgement page in the works of other authors, I have often felt that it must be the most difficult part of a book to write. Can you possibly thank all the people who helped make a journey possible? Won't someone get lost in the shuffle? I never envied an author's task when writing those portions of the book. And now I am in that position. Let's hope I can do just as well as they have.

To begin, I would like to thank L'Arche International for putting together such a wonderful organization, helping those who are so often left behind. It is wonderful to have been involved with them for the past few years. More specifically, L'Arche Mobile is owed endless gratitude for helping give my year of running a greater purpose above and beyond simply running a marathon each weekend.

Anne, my best friend, you made this year possible. Your countless hours of promotion, empathetic ear and trouble-shooting helped keep my spirits buoyant when times were tough. If we had ever had to make that 24-hour straight road trip to Denver and back, I know you would have made it fun.

My mom and dad, who never quite understood where their son got his particular bout of crazy (and I am not just referring to this year), never once wavered in their support of my task. My entire family is owed thanks as they were both cheerleaders and promoters while filling the ears of all with tales of my travels.

The Georgetown Running Company was extremely helpful to me by providing both gear and advice. Super Shuttle was integral in returning my

SEE DANE RUN

Tanya,

Always chase your dreams!

_2011_

One Man
52 Weekends, 52 Marathons

Dane E. Rauschenberg

First Published 2008

Copyright 2008 by Dane E. Rauschenberg

ISBN: 978-0-9683158-5-9

Library and Archives Canada Cataloguing in Publication

Rauschenberg, Dane E., 1976-
    See Dane run : one man, 52 weekends, 52 marathons / Dane E. Rauschenberg.

ISBN 978-0-9683158-5-9
    1. Rauschenberg, Dane E., 1976-. 2. Marathon running. 3. Runners

(Sports)--United States--Biography. I. Title.

GV1061.15.R38A3 2008   796.42'52092   C2008-907567-6

Published by The Experience Publishers
www.experiencebooks.ca
Ottawa, Ontario, Canada
1-877-755-5155
michelle@experiencebooks.ca

Cover Design by Jacqueline Vinkle
Cover Images Credits
Globe: © Alex Staroseltsev | Dreamstime.com, Road Scene: © Leonardo Tumonis | Dreamstime.com

weary carcass from the airport to my home every weekend and allowed me to avoid long lines for taxis. To both of these companies, I extend my heartfelt thanks.

Patrick at The Stick (www.thestick.com) helped rub away soreness at every expo I saw him and Terrel Hale used his expertise in massage therapy to heal countless sore muscles, aches and pains. Without a doubt, the year was made easier because of both of their efforts.

Joe's Pizza and Pasta in Arlington Virginia helped feed my never empty belly all year. One would think I would get sick of eating pasta three times a week, but with this fine cuisine I never tired of trips to Joe's stores!

Mike and Ed at Road ID helped give me and my loved ones peace of mind by making sure I was always well-identified. DC Access helped get my website off the ground and AllSportCentral handled the donation module. With all of their help, my job was made that much easier.

Friends from the past and countless new acquaintances I met on the way during 2006 made sure I never felt alone on my journey. From race directors to random strangers, this adventure was every bit a success because of your caring and kindness, as it was because of my own running.

And to all of those runners and walkers out there, who always made me smile as you laced up your shoes and tightened your water belts, even when we never exchanged a single word, I thank you. The world is a better place the more runners we have in it.

Dane Rauschenberg's account of his personal triumph, all the hard work, the long hours, and the solitary effort is a must read for anyone who has ever dreamed of doing the impossible. It is an honor to be asked to write the forward to this journal of one man's determination to fulfill a lifelong dream.

To run a marathon takes a certain kind of courage, a commitment to long, often solitary training runs in all conditions, a singularity of purpose and not just a little bit of faith. To run 52 marathons in 52 weeks is an order of magnitude of difference. The focus and determination, the flexibility to take what the marathon gives you and the faith to go on, to keep on when every part of you wants to stop this is the mark of the true long distance runner.

I have run many marathons in my life. At one time as an elite runner and now as competitive masters runner with a commitment to giving it my best every time I set out. No matter what one's status is as a runner, the miles hurt each of us in much the same way, and equally, those same miles raise us up to be our best in much the same way. The people we meet, the sights we see, the things we learn about who we are and in the end, why we are here, are valuable not only to each of us individually but to anyone who has ever set out on a long journey of unknown result.

So put on your good running shoes, settle back in your comfortable chair and go on a journey with a remarkable runner, a remarkable man....Dane Rauschenberg

Dick Beardsley

Dick Beardsley is the 3rd fastest American born runner and the 5th fastest U.S. men's marathon time in history. Best known for his 1982 Boston Marathon "Duel in the Sun" with Alberto Salazar, Dick is also a two-time Olympic Trials Marathon qualifier. He is a two-time winner and course record holder of the Grandma's Marathon in Duluth, Minnesota and has won the London and Napa Valley marathons.

Table of Contents

Introduction

You're doing what?

The story I have to share is about how I ran one marathon every weekend for an entire calendar year, a quest I dubbed "Fiddy2" (a common mispronunciation of the word "fifty-two".) The focus of my running was to benefit the Mobile, Alabama chapter of L'Arche; an international organization that works with mentally and physically challenged individuals. Helping L'Arche Mobile was an integral part of the answer to the question I am most often asked when others learn about what I did in 2006: Why? That question, while so short, always provokes the longest answers.

The shortest and most truthful answer I can give is: Why not? The driving force behind many of the things I have done in my life is a desire to push myself to do something I have never attempted before, and a desire to push myself to do something no one has ever attempted before. But the real genesis of the idea to do something many would call "crazy" is more complex than "why not?"

I have always aspired to maintain a high level of physical fitness. And, having traveled very little in my life before college, I wanted to see the United States, as well as the world. New places, new faces and new experiences always make my pulse race. In addition, I found, in the days before Fiddy2, that when it comes to long distance running, my body could handle far more than the average person's. It will become clear how the confluence of these desires and abilities pushed me towards my plan for 2006, with surprises at every turn.

It was not until I was in the midst of planning Fiddy2 that I learned L'Arche Mobile even existed. Finding out about this wonderful organization and deciding to make it the focus of Fiddy2 was just one of those happy twists of fate.

So, when I realized that no simple answer could possibly explain the myriad reasons why I decided to do what I did in 2006, the idea of writing it all down came to me. The funny thing is that, as the year went by, I found out that what was happening around me as I traveled to different places, and met new people, was going to be far more exciting than just a long story about myself. It became clear to me that because of my unique experience in 2006, I would be able to share with many a perspective few could. The book could not simply be about marathons. Of course, I will describe the marathons I ran and what their courses were like. If nothing else, this book can be used by runners as a guide on courses, race directors and sundry other items pertaining to the races and the events surrounding them.

But more important, I hope to give you a glimpse into all of the wonderful (and some of the not-so-wonderful) people and events that crossed my path while I raced 1,362.4 miles. If I entertain, that is wonderful. If I inspire, then that is even better.

Just do not get me started on air travel.

Beginnings

One of the joys of running, and more specifically racing, is that you know in advance there is a predetermined beginning and definitive end. While other sports have a clock that shows you that time is escaping, running has one that counts up, piling onto a total that started at zero. You do not lose time in a race; rather, you gain it. And you hope, when all is said and done, that you have gained as little time as possible.

I have always been involved in sports. Good in some, better in others, and by hustle alone, not picked last for a few. Most of those sports involved a ball of some sort. I grew up in America and football, baseball and soccer were what I was raised on (basketball being one that falls into that Thank God for Hustle category.) Running, more often than not, was what I did at practice as either conditioning or punishment. Out of shape? Run. Failed to perform the drill correctly? Run.

As early as elementary school I knew I was "quick" not "fast." I would often compete in the local Hershey Track and Field games held in my hometown of Titusville, Pennsylvania. These games, set up to promote physical fitness in young children, were started the year before I was born. It seems we are fighting a losing battle against juvenile obesity but I know I personally enjoyed the games. Every year, I signed up for all sorts of athletic events, from the softball toss to a myriad of track events. In eighth grade, my last year of eligibility for these games, I shattered my collarbone playing baseball just a few short weeks before the qualifying events in Titusville; I was left with no more attempts to fulfill my dream of flying at incredible speeds.

However, long before that day, I routinely was reminded that I was never going to be a sprinter. I would finish in the bottom half of the field for these short dashes. And running more than one lap (for the longer events) seemed absolutely ridiculous to me at the time. Once in high school, I tried to figure out if perhaps my stride was wrong or my arms swayed the wrong way. I studied the fast kids. Those who could run like gazelles with limited effort were always the bane of my existence. Where were my fast-twitch muscle fibers? Why couldn't I accelerate like that? But no matter how much effort I poured into getting faster, I was at best "quick." In sports, I rarely got caught from behind, but I most assuredly wasn't going to fly by anyone or make coaches dig out their stopwatches. Regardless, I played sports because, well, I love them. In spite of limited talent, I played on.

That quickness helped me steal bases in high school, but, as one baseball advertisement said, chicks dig the long ball, so when I got to high school I hung up my baseball cleats. When it came to football, I had a moderately successful career as a wide receiver, mostly because I could catch just about anything. With tiny hands for someone 6'1", I have no idea how this is possible. Yet in spite of my love of the old pigskin, it turns out the sport I was best at in high school was swimming.

Unlike many of my other chlorine-smelling green-haired friends, I came to swimming late in the game. I had taken swimming lessons when I was quite young at a local pool just a few blocks away from where I grew up. However, learning how to swim and subsequently enjoying being in the water did not immediately make me want to join the YMCA swim team like all of my friends. Swimming is what I did for fun. In the sun! Why would I want to swim *laps* in a *building?*

Every year on my birthday, my mother's parents bought me a season pass to the pool. With my birthday on May 31st (feel free to send cards) it was always just in time for the summer swim season. My mother called it her summertime babysitter. From noon until five (home for a quick dinner) and then back again all evening, a host of friends and I would play endless games of tag. Because we had to avoid the lifeguards with their quick-draw whistles and "No run-ning!" shouts, we soon mastered the fast-walk. In fact, because of those tag days, I am pretty sure I could make the Olympics with the rest of those goofy-looking "roggers" or "running joggers." (And if you are offended when I call it goofy-looking, then you have never seen one of those races. Take a peek and get back to me.) But this experience at the pool was not one that translated over to the swim team as I grew up.

Not until just before tenth grade when one of the lifeguards who had been on the Titusville swim team mentioned that it was a shame I was not on that team, did I even give it a thought. I mentioned it to my mother and she said he was right. The guys on the swim team were all kids whom I would often out-swim in our games at the pool. Surely, I would have no trouble beating them in a race. But then I remembered those flip-turn things and how im-possible they looked. After telling the lifeguard I was interested in joining the team but had no idea about technique, he gave me a few pointers. I decided to spend a few evening swims away from my friends, who were playing the low-key version of our afternoon all-sprint tag, and began working on my flip-turns. It was easy as pie! Swim towards the wall, throw the legs over, turn around, and push off. Wait. Hold on. Where is the wall? Why am I still facing the wall? Nevertheless, I kept trying and eventually was able to get a passable flip turn down.

I had an uneventful first year on the team. Placed well down the chart for the majority of the year where I struggled with both the flip-turn and the start, I still enjoyed myself. Of course, for a sprinter there are few things more im-portant than a flip-turn or a start so you can see why I languished. And while my flip-turn improved throughout high school, I actually never acquired more than an average start. No matter. I was having fun.

In the last swim meet of my first year, we were swimming an inferior team. Unlike ball sports where anything can happen, in swimming (much like track) you know how fast someone swims and whether they are better than you. Rarely are there big drops in time from one meet to the next. Therefore, in situations where you know that the score is going to get out of hand quickly and there really is no need to embarrass the other school (sort of a pre-emp-tive mercy rule) swimmers will swim events or strokes they usually do not swim. This policy helps keep the score closer and (I found out later) is a tool coaches use to find hidden talents. When I discovered my coach had put me in the 500-meter event (sort of the swimming version of the mile or two mile run), I groaned. Twenty lengths of the pool! Sprinters are known whiners when it comes to anything over 100 meters. And even though at that time I was not a particularly good sprinter, I was enjoying not being a horribly bad long distance guy as well.

Well, long story short I ended up swimming the 500 meter in a time just a few seconds off of our school record. Whoops. Now I had done it. The swim coach smiled and said, "Guess what you're swimming next year?" I vowed to quit. Only half-jokingly, mind you.

Seeded dead last in the 50-meter at our local district meet; I was pleased to beat the sole guy in my heat. In fact, I was able to best a few other guys in the heat above me and finished something like third to dead last. I hoped this meteoric rise in the sprinter ranks would make my coach forget about my 500 time. However, it was not that particular coach who I had to make forget about my times. You see, in the revolving carousel of swimming coaches I had during high school, each year brought with it a new swimming coach. In fact, when we weren't able to secure a new coach for my junior year, our high school principal volunteered to do the job. For a kid like me, who I liked to call a white-collar juvenile delinquent (I caused a smidgen of harmless trouble in high school) having your principal as your coach was just about the most horrid thing I could fathom. Turns out, Terry Funk is one of the best coaches I have ever had in any sport.

Funk, a collegiate swimmer at Penn State, is just an all-around nice guy. His family is nice, far too good-looking, and just a damn pleasure to be around. This I see now. But in high school he was my coach. A coach who was also my principal. He was the enemy. Well, not really. I actually enjoyed him then nearly as much as I do now and without a doubt he was the coach for whom I wanted to do my best. Yet never once was he anything but positive. So even though I felt terrible when I let myself down (I am my own worse critic), it was Mr. Funk I hated to disappoint. Even when he found out about my 500 time and told me I was going to be a distance guy.

Jerk.

In my junior year we fielded a much stronger team than we had the previous season. However, the unexpected thing for me personally was how, even though I was our main distance guy, I became one of our top sprinters. This oddity was definitely one we would begin to use to our advantage in my junior year and even more so in my senior year. Using me both as a sprinter and a distance guy, our coach could play a little chess.

And, to be honest, I enjoyed being different. It set me apart and made me feel like I was helping the team. Swimming is one of those sports where you truly compete alone. I liked that. If I did not accomplish what I set out to accomplish then I knew the blame was only on me. Without a doubt, the team's overall performance made me happy but it was nice to know I had done everything I possibly could to help the team win. It is surprising that I did not see the corollary to track sooner.

Having succeeded in becoming an integral part of our swim team, I felt I had earned my team hat. So, before the swim season was over, I asked my mother if she would buy me one. Gladly, she brought home my hat. But instead of an embroidered "Titusville Rockets Swimming" on the front, my mother had inadvertently purchased one that read "Titusville Rockets Track & Field." Apparently, a Track hat had made its way into the Swimming hat pile and my mother had not noticed until I pointed it out. She volunteered to take the hat back and get me the proper hat.

I guess I must have felt a new challenge rising inside me. I had been thinking about track; how during the spring my buddies were not around to have fun with because most of them were down either running or throwing. I looked at my mom and, as with most things in my life, made a rather quick decision that would impact me for a lifetime.

"Don't worry about it." I said. "I will just run track."

2

Running

I knew I was not a sprinter. That was a given. So, with the decision to join the track team in mind, I approached the distance coach and asked him where he thought I might fit. Brent Henderson, unlike a lot of coaches in those days who would assign practices they themselves never could have done on their best day, not only coached track and cross-country but could whip most of our butts in any race. We had no choice but to respect that, especially since our distance team was petty darn good. How good we were, I would soon learn.

Coming off the swim season, I was in the best shape of my life. I knew I was not in running shape, but felt my lungs would help me hold out until my legs caught up. In fact, with the lungs of a swimmer, I figured I at least had an advantage over other rookies. Too bad the only other rookies were ninth graders. Moreover, these rookies could run. I soon found out that I was not even close to being ready to hang with the fastest guys on the team.

One of our top runners, Mac Knapp, was extremely gifted and dedicated. Often Coach Henderson would give Mac free rein to take the distance guys out on a practice run. Mac would lead us out on training runs that were at least as hard as the coach would have ordered.

Track season begins officially in March for the Titusville Rockets. March in Northwestern Pennsylvania usually means snow. And tons of it. So on one of my very first runs with the team, Mac, an eventual state champion in the two-mile, led us up and down hills, floundering through wet, deep snow and just about making me never want to run again. My lungs were fine. But my legs were shot. Of course, there was no question of whether I would quit the team but I wondered if I had perhaps bitten off more than I could chew. Everyone else seemed like they were fine with the workout but then again, everyone else was also on the cross-country team. Five-kilometer races and the like (unthinkable distances to me at the time) were the norm for these guys. And so, apparently, was being taken by Mac out on the backcountry roads to die.

But I stuck with it.

Now, it would be a lie to tell you I remember much about my first event. I do recall running scared once the gun went off in fear of that dreaded last place finish. I took off from the start and just kept running. With one lap down, I have a vague recollection of trying to figure out where everyone else was. When I turned onto the homestretch and the final one hundred meters, I realized I was going to win. I was pleased and shocked. It was a great way to start the season.

Before I knew it, I had played my senior season of football, had an excellent end to my swimming career and it was time for track again.

To this day, Coach Henderson says that maybe once in a lifetime does a coach get to be involved with a team as utterly dominating as this one. In fact, one of the biggest upsets of the year was the time we traveled to the McDowell Invitational in Erie, Pennsylvania. Sporting a graduating class of 453 that year, McDowell had never lost the invitational it hosted. When we left that Saturday evening, their loss total was now "one." Tiny Titusville, with a graduating class of only 144, had felled the Goliath.

With the year winding down, I qualified for the state meet and watched Mac take the two-mile championship (and some other classmates do very well across the board as well) and capped off an excellent senior year. But with the state meet finished, running competitively in college never crossed my mind. All I could think about were the walk-on football tryouts at Penn State.

My decision to further my education at Penn State was in no small way influenced by my desire to play football for Joe Paterno. I knew my chances were iffy at best to fulfill this dream (remember that whole "being slow" thing I mentioned before) but they were much closer to zero if I went to any of the smaller schools which had expressed some interest in me. Fortunately, I rarely let facts deter me from attempting to conquer the world or at least, small towns in central Pennsylvania. Unfortunately, a few days before I would start my freshman year at Penn State, fate stepped in. For the third time in my life, in a pickup game of football with some friends (rather ironic), my collarbone failed me.

With my dreams of walking on to the Penn State football team put on hold, I started college. Besides the occasional intramural game here and there, my life was more or less devoid of participatory sports. I was out of shape and unmotivated. I recall that running just a few (and I mean very few) miles became a chore.

Perhaps I can blame the collarbone and the extended layover from sports and exercise (the break had left the bone in pieces like a jigsaw puzzle) or perhaps I will blame college food, but this was a low period in my life for physical fitness. In spite of this, I knew I was at Penn State for many reasons and one of them was to try and play at Beaver Stadium. I decided to give the tryouts another shot.

I did not make the team. No storybook ending for our author. However, I learned an invaluable lesson about life, as well as finding out something about myself. It was then that I developed what would become my mantra: there are many things in this world you cannot do. Trying is not one of them.

I do not believe that we can do anything we want as long as we give it our best. To believe that, you must either have a much sunnier disposition than I, or be able to delude yourself. You see we definitely do have limits. There are hurdles that, for one reason or another, we will never get over. And honestly, I have no problem with that.

What I do have a problem with is accepting that truth and allowing it to deter me from attempting to achieve. Fortunately, humans have been blessed with selective memory and a distorted sense of reality when it comes to what they can or should try to achieve. We constantly strive to succeed even when we know we will fail.

Failure is good. We learn far more from failure than we do from success. We are not good at everything we try. But some of us are able ignore the facts and forge on regardless.

What I learned about myself was that I do not accept failure. Ever. My mother, who of course loves me and will therefore always says complimentary things about me has said, "Do not tell Dane he cannot do something unless you want to see it get done." (She will also tell you I am a pain in the ass.)

So when I failed at football tryouts, and was asked to try out for the rugby team, I gave it a shot. I made the team but played infrequently in my two semesters on the Penn State team. I finished college on time, in spite of changing majors in the middle of my junior year, and prioritizing time spent with my girlfriend. So, taking eight classes in my last semester just to graduate, I put sports behind me once again.

When I entered law school a year later, I had yet to lose the extra weight I had put on in college. Enough was enough; one day early in my first year I decided to go for a run. I barely survived 3 miles. When I saw another law school classmate out for a jog, I figured I would have to talk to her the next day. And talk we did.

Besides the fact that she was a fellow Penn Stater and we actually shared mutual friends (small world indeed), I learned she was training for the Boston Marathon. I was far from intrigued. Marginally interested would be a better phrase. But I wanted a running partner, and Kristy and I became fast friends. Never had I even contemplated such a thing as running a marathon. Running with Kristy, hearing her dedication and also wanting to taste athletics again, got me excited. The seeds were planted

A few miles here and a few miles there, Kristy began working me into shape. Meanwhile, I decided to play rugby for my law school at the club level. I felt I had enough skill to at least play with the guys. Heck, we were all out-of-shape law students.

9

Kristy signed us up for a half-marathon.

"You owe me 35 dollars," she said. That was how I learned I was going to race 13.1 miles. I had no idea how I was going to do. But, as I was determined not to crash and burn, Kristy and I ran stride for stride for the majority of the race. Kristy finally let me take off with just a few miles to go to see what I could do. I finished with a time in the high 1:30s. I was still incredibly pleased. I had run 13.1 miles! The world was my oyster.

But that oyster would no longer contain rugby. Just a few days before finals started, I got pulled down awkwardly in a match and bent my elbow the wrong way. Four torn tendons, a ripped bicep and one dislocated elbow made certain my days of playing rugby were over. After my arm healed, I attempted to give the game another shot, but I could tell my tentativeness was going to get me injured. Therefore, rugby was done. Running would become my exercise savior.

As law school passed, I slimmed down and began to feel fit again. Continuing with my streak of luck in first time events, I entered a 5k sponsored by the law school and was able to take first place. The time is so embarrassing I will not even print it here. But the fact remains I had yet another "victory" under my belt and had my sights on more. Back at my dorm I called Kristy. After telling her I had won, I blurted out, "I want to run a marathon!" She sounded so excited that I thought she would burst. I think she was just happy to have a training partner.

My training began to intensify as I continued to build up stamina and speed. Kristy ran her Boston Marathon and that only further whetted my appetite. I had tracked her online using those new-fangled timing chips and cheered at every 5k split as it popped up on the screen. (In 2000 chip timing had only been around for a few years and the idea of following someone online was just about the coolest thing ever.)

My training and mileage increased. However, an injury from the past began to be a problem. After sustaining a knock to my leg while playing high school football, I had developed a rather large calcium deposit in my right quadriceps muscle. With every knee bend, it popped. I had been dealing with this abnormality for seven years; I was actually quite used to the pain.

But I had never before put in the type of mileage on the roads that I was now. Not only was the quadriceps hurting, but the other leg began to feel discomfort as well because of the compensation factor. Finally, it was more than I could handle.

Obviously something needed to be done if I wanted to continue running. I weighed my options. It was clear the pain would not go away if I continued to run. And it was clear I could not run a marathon with this calcium deposit in my leg. And I was going to run a marathon.

The doctor prescribed surgery. My training, physical fitness, and goals would once again be put on hold as I went under the knife in early 2001. Three broken collarbones, a severely injured arm and now surgery were all threatening to derail any thoughts I had to run a marathon or succeed athletically post-high school. Even those who never give up can become disheartened by these setbacks.

As I was wheeled into the operating room, I will admit I was amongst their ranks.

3

Marathons

The surgery went smoothly. Before long, I was running again and determined to run that first 26.2 miles.

With the leg on the mend and the miles beginning to pile up again, I had to choose a marathon. Spring had rapidly turned into summer, and I did not want to wait too long to get out on the roads and see what I could do in that fabled distance. I knew I wanted a race with a low registration fee and one close to home (I was still a law student with no cash.) Kristy suggested the Harrisburg Marathon. At this point in my running I did just about anything Kristy said, so the 2001 Harrisburg Marathon was going to be where I started my running career over again.

Perhaps I had the arrogance of a former athlete, and a certain ignorance of what it takes to successfully complete 26.2 miles or possibly with law school, an internship and a job, I did not have as much time to train as would be ideal, but my effort before the marathon left much to be desired. I thought that my strong will alone would make up for what I lacked in training and endurance. Hadn't I successfully completed a half marathon with tons of energy left in the tank? I had done a 16-mile training run carrying a cell phone and talking to a friend for most of the run. Surely I could just tack on a few miles, run super fast and count the marathon as another thing in life I had successfully conquered.

As I drove to the race the morning of, I was a little chilly. But I knew that it was supposed to warm up during the day. At the time, this idea pleased me. I am not a fan of being cold; even the slight briskness of the morning was not something I wanted to deal with. I figured I had run in the heat before and it always felt good. Breaking a sweat makes me feel like I am actually working hard so I had no reason to believe it would be any different on this morning.

I parked my car and meandered towards the start. About 300 runners were milling around as well. This seemed like a large crowd to me for a race in Harrisburg. There were all shapes and sizes of runners in all sorts of apparel. Wearing a half-long-sleeved cotton t-shirt, biker shorts under soccer shorts, regular sunglasses that you would wear to the beach, a beaded necklace and shoes which probably were not meant to run anything longer than a 10k, I felt like I fit in. Looking back at the only race photo I have of the time, I want to grab Young Dane and shake him. "What in the hell were you thinking?" I would like to say. "Cotton t-shirt? On a day that was going to be hot?" But hindsight is, well, you know. Lessons learned the hard way are the best learned.

The race started and I told any runner who was near me that this was my first marathon. They all cordially wished me good luck and immediately made me feel like I was one of them. The first few miles passed by and I felt pretty good. The course was relatively flat, I was hanging in a pack of what seemed like fast runners and I was doing well.

We turned towards the Susquehanna River and a blast of wind hit us head-on. I had been trying to use runners to block the wind but they had pulled away. Now alone, I put my head down and pushed forward. I went through the first nine miles a little tired but faster than I thought I would. I was hoping for a 3:30 but my misguided calculations (which were not factoring in fatigue or a variety of other circumstances) had me well below that time.

I went through the half in about 1:33. Wow! If I ran faster in the second half I could have a shot at a sub-3 marathon in my first ever 26.2 miler. That would impress Kristy! But soon I began to slow down. My energy dropped precipitously and I grew more and more thirsty. I was drinking at every aid stop, so I could not figure out why I was losing energy so fast.

I passed mile 16, which to that point had been my longest continuous run.

Something was wrong. I definitely did not feel like I had another 10 miles in me. I tried to put these thoughts out of my mind and focus on other events. In the first few hours after the planes had crashed into the Twin Towers two months previously, I had laced up my shoes and gone for a run through my neighborhood. I couldn't tolerate being near a television. I found solace in my running. Here, I was in control. I could handle this. With no friends or family in NYC, I knew I was lucky. I only had me to worry about. And me I could handle.

These same thoughts were in my mind two months later when I started a hill at mile 19. Then there was a pop. Followed by a shooting pain in my knee. Followed by me crumbling to the ground. I was able to fall to the side of the road and into some leaves. The searing pain left me as rapidly as it had hit but the damage was done. I was losing energy, I was extremely thirsty, and my knee hurt. Not badly enough to make me quit but definitely enough to make me wonder if I had properly healed from the surgery just a few months prior. So now, on top of everything, I had the mental monkey playing games in my mind. There are few things worse than the mental monkey. Once the mental monkey gets in your head, it takes a stick most of us cannot wield to shoo him away.

The next seven miles consisted of me either jogging or shuffling. More and more people passed me. The dreams of a sub-3 hour race passed. Then 3:15, then 3:30. Friends who had been waiting for me at the finish began to think they had arrived too late. Had I run a 2:45 and was searching for them, they wondered?

A 4:00 finish slipped by. In between water stops I begged runners who passed me for water off of their fuel belts. On reflection, I am absolutely astounded I had the audacity to ask fellow runners to share their own liquids. But they all gladly helped me out. I think they could see I was in bad shape.

Determined to salvage the tiniest bit of dignity, I bucked up to finish under 4:15. That last half mile is one of the longest distances I have ever covered. I passed a few people as I picked up speed and this soothed my ego some in spite of grumbles under the breath of some runners. They seemed to be saying, "Why sprint now?" I am sure it was all in my mind. Regardless, nothing anyone said would have mattered to me at that point. I had to use the little energy I had left to get myself across the line. Finally, four hours, twelve

14

minutes and seven seconds after I started my first marathon ever I was done, 159th out of 238 runners. Well-positioned in the bottom third. Few things could have gone more wrong.

My friends ushered me to a first aid tent and I lay down flat on the table. The first aid people could see that I was severely dehydrated. They got some fluids in me and kept me talking. I tried to tell my friends what had gone wrong but I did not know for sure. I had grown tired. I had grown thirsty. I had hurt my leg somehow. But I had not expected to run a 1:33 first half and then a 2:39 second half! Perhaps the marathon distance was not for me after all.

As I came to grips with this possibility, I realized I was feeling well enough to begin to mosey back to my car. Still sipping fluids and walking gingerly I had a heavy mind and heart for various reasons. First, I was not looking forward to calling my parents and letting them know I had not done as well as I had hoped. Always supportive, they would never make me feel bad for falling short in my goals, but still I hated telling them. In addition, in the days leading up to the marathon, one of my favorite people in the world had taken ill.

My grandmother had gone to the hospital one week before the marathon for a routine check-up and while under the eyes of her physician had suffered a stroke. Her condition had been deteriorating all week. Small periods of lucidity allowed glimmers of hope to my mother and her siblings. When I called my parents I wanted to get the marathon talk out of the way as quickly as possible. My dad answered the phone and I told him I had not done as well as I liked. He offered his condolences and reminded me it was a tough race. I asked if Mom was around. He said she was not. It was Sunday midmorning; there would be no reason for my mom to be anywhere else but at home with my dad. I immediately knew.

"Grandma?" I asked.

"She's gone," my Dad said. "Early this morning."

I hung up the phone and wept.

4

Planting a Seed

After my first marathon I suffered nagging leg injuries and took a sabbatical from running. My third year of law school went by with a smattering of running here and there but nothing spectacular. I was spending my time taking classes, working for the district attorney's office and studying for the bar. Before I knew it, I had graduated from law school, taken the bar exam, and was clerking for a judge in Erie, Pennsylvania. I began to wish to get into shape again. At least, while running itself had been on the back burner, I had supplemented my fitness with a brief stint in amateur boxing. Once I began working for the court, I decided that I needed to retire from the sweet science. I simply could not go into court sporting a black eye or missing tooth. But the boxing had kept me in pretty good shape and when the running bug bit again, at least I was not starting from scratch.

I decided to take another crack at running a marathon. This time I promised myself to prepare properly. I trained harder, put in the requisite twenty-mile runs and, come race day, I was primed. I cruised through the first half in 1:28 and thought for sure that I would go sub-3. Not bad for a second attempt, I thought.

But it was not to be. Mile by mile my energy again wore down. I was forced to walk a few times and drink as much as I could in the last few miles as I was once again completely dry in the mouth. When I crossed the line, I had made nearly a 45-minute improvement to 3:29 but had turned the final lap of this two-lap course into a clinic of what not to do. My girlfriend at the time could tell I was severely unhappy. Besides the obvious disappointment of not meeting my racing goal, something else was nagging at me but I could not put my finger on it.

That day passed and the race season in Erie continued. I ran other races here and there and posted some times I was relatively pleased with. After my clerkship ended, my job search took me to Washington, D.C. I remembered the Marine Corps Marathon was in D.C. Perhaps I could give this marathon thing one last shot. I did a quick search on the Internet; the race had long since sold out. The only way I could get in was to run for a charity.

I researched charities and found St. Jude's. As is usual with me, when I get an idea I run with it full-speed ahead and by that night I was speaking to someone about being a St. Jude's Hero. I needed to raise $1500 in order to run (or pay the remainder come race day); I set about it right away. I soon realized that either it is very hard to fundraise or I suck at it. Thank goodness for the generosity of a few because I barely made the minimum amount needed before I would have had to dip into my own pockets to cover the rest.

I was taking the race seriously this time. I joined a running club in DC, got a marathon-training plan from a well-known magazine and set to it. With a long run of 22 miles in a good time in warm weather on a training run, and a plethora of other good days underneath me, I was assured this would be the year I broke through.

But not only did I not get faster, I actually got slower. I climbed the hill to the Iwo Jima Memorial and put in a time of 3:31 exactly. I soon found myself in the cascade of my shower, wondering if perhaps the marathon was just not my distance. I seemed to do rather well in the half marathon and then it fell apart. The worst part was this time I had taken the training seriously, had put in the requisite long hard runs, followed the training programs and still ended up with disappointing results. I only had one more marathon to go and then I could call the whole marathon idea a failed experiment and move on.

The decision to run two marathons within three weeks of each other was made before I even toed the line at the Marine Corps Marathon. Always frugal, I decided to give the next marathon a shot even though my last result had been so disappointing. My desire not to waste the money already spent on the registration fee was one of the best decisions I have ever made.

Nothing pointed towards this day being any different than my previous races. In fact, the Marathon in the Parks in Bethesda, Maryland was a hillier course than I have ever run and with temperatures below freezing the course was covered in black ice. Throw in the short rest from the last marathon, no expectations that I would excel and wearing new clothing which I had not planned on wearing (the starting temperature was 29 degrees; three weeks earlier at Marine Corps it had been 50 degrees warmer) and this was no recipe for success.

But as the race wore on I stayed consistent. I still took the first half too fast but I figured I was going to go down swinging. The pavement was slippery in spots as we went up and down the trail that wound through some gorgeous parks in Bethesda. I kept waiting for the inevitable crash of energy.

It never came. I slowed my pace as I neared the finish and was a little bothered when a number of people passed me in the last few miles but I was hanging tough. Up one long last hill with the crisp air cutting into us, we ran through an underpass and out onto the city streets. About 100 yards away was the finish line. I pushed as hard as I could. I cruised over in 3:19:05, a personal record! As I scarfed some homemade chili I could not believe how fast I had run (for me anyway). I realized I had the cold weather to thank. I simply had not sweated as much as I had in my previous marathons and therefore was nowhere near as dehydrated. Every marathon I had run before this had been run in very warm temperatures. I had simply not hydrated enough in the previous races. I felt like I had a new lease on this marathon thing.

The previous summer, at a high school ten-year reunion, a friend told me she was running her first marathon in Phoenix.

"If you happen to be in the area you should come out and run with me," Jenny had said.

As I drove home from today's marathon the thought occurred to me that I would never just "be" in Phoenix for no reason; I would have to deliberately take her up on her invitation. I confirmed she would still be running, signed up for the marathon and bought a plane ticket that night.

Over the next month or so I did not run much. I felt a little under the weather, the holidays loomed and I was simply taking it easy as winter set in. I had no intention to do anything that special in Phoenix but run another marathon and start my year off right.

Jenny's husband dropped us off a few blocks from the start. We chatted a bit while we waited for the sun to come up and shuffled to the start. The slightly chilly air temp made me smile: I hoped I would not experience the heat that had been the bane of my existence in three of my other four events. As I stood in the first corral I had my first brush with celebrity in a race. Roger Craig, the former San Francisco 49ers running back was within arm's reach. The gun started, we took off and I wished Roger good luck. I was totally hoping I would smoke him and started out fast.

About 4 miles into the race, natured called and I ducked into a porta-potty. As I emerged the 3:10 pace group (the time I needed to qualify for Boston) passed by. I was a little miffed I was that far ahead of that pace group this early in the race but glad I had stopped to use the bathroom and decided to fall in line with them. I didn't expect to finish with them but it was worth a shot.

Miles ticked by. The group thinned. Around mile 19 I saddled up to the pace leader and told him I desperately wanted a 3:10 and felt that I might just get it. I did not feel as tired as I had in previous marathons. He told me to down the power gel I was holding, grab a drink of water, and run with him. He would get me there.

I began to get nervous around mile 23 or 24. It was now just me and the pace leader. Everyone else had either fallen back or surged forward. He did everything short of grabbing my arm whenever I surged and told me to stay with him. Mile 25 appeared and passed. I was really beginning to get tired. I was no longer talking. I was running with eyes half-closed. I knew I had the energy but simply could not stand the suspense. It was going to be close. Mile 26 was a blur. The clock appeared. The pace leader turned full sideways and like a drill sergeant yelled at me, "You are going to Boston!" I crossed in 3:09:49.

Seconds after I finished I hugged him, thanking him for his help. Tears stained my cheeks. I had been trying to accomplish this little goal to honor my grandmother for three years and I had finally done it.

A volunteer asked, "Are you okay?"

I told her, "I'm fine. I did this run in memory of my gramma."

The woman teared up and said, "Well, now you've got me crying too!"

I snaked my way through the meeting area and back out onto the course. Jenny would still be out there and might want a running partner. I found her around mile 25. She was grateful for the orange I brought her and we ran the rest of the way in together. She finished in a very respectable sub 4:15 time and was happy.

On the plane ride home, my brain was in overdrive. I had finally done what I had set out to do. I could sit back and relax. Pick a marathon here and there and simply enjoy. I am sure I smiled like an idiot the whole way home.

Once back, my brother mentioned that there was a marathon in Tampa, where he lived.

"You should run so you can visit me."

Only a few weeks away, so I figured, why not? And since there was no logical way I could be expected to run as fast as I had in Phoenix, I decided to sign up for the PT Cruiser Challenge. This event consisted of a 15k at 7:30 am on Saturday, a 5k two hours later and then a marathon the next day at 6 am.

I was shocked to find I not only survived this contest but also ended up besting every other competitor who had attempted all three events. Running with a "For Grandpa" attached to my clothing, it was a fitting tribute to my grandfather who had passed away almost a year to the day of the marathon. My mother joked that my grandmother had the last laugh, as "her" marathon in Phoenix was faster than the one I had run here by about 30 seconds. I smiled and remembered crossing the finish line in Tampa pointing up to the sky to both of them while also pointing at the sign on my chest.

This time on the flight home thoughts went a different way. I had run the PT Cruiser Challenge instead of just the marathon because I had heard it was not good for the body to run more than a few marathons a year. In fact, doing so more or less guaranteed you would never get any faster. But here in this race, while hardly setting the world on fire with my 3:10, I had been almost able to equal my best time ever while also running pretty hard the day before.

I was pretty sure that no matter what training I did, I was never going to be a super fast marathon runner. I was already 28, had shown throughout my life that fast running was really not my forte, and I was not about to quit work and do nothing but run in order to get to that possible plateau. However, now I seemed to have some more evidence to prove a sneaking suspicion that what I was in fact cut out for was running a lot with little rest. At this point I honestly knew next to nothing about marathons, ultra marathons, the history of running or anything else. I just had a hunch.

In 2003, one month after my second marathon in Erie, I had decided to try an event that at the time seemed to me just ridiculous. The Presque Isle Personal Endurance Classic was a running event wherein people traversed a one-mile loop as fast as they could in order to see how far they could go in a 12 hour period. Starting at 6:30 am participants had exactly 12 hours to accumulate as much mileage as possible. I'd had next to no expectations going into this event of doing anything out of the ordinary.

To keep me motivated I had taken to asking people to donate to the American Cancer Society for every mile I ran (my grandfather whom I mentioned earlier, contracted and was swiftly taken from us by cancer just a month after I finished this race.) I figured I could make it sixty miles in 12 hours and that is what I told most people. I didn't tell anyone that I had another idea brewing.

When the Classic started it was a chilly and slightly rainy day. It was easy to run on this super flat loop with just a smidgen of an incline leading from the paved road to a well-worn trail on the backside. I would get to know this trail pretty intimately over the next 12 hours. For now, I was just trying to not think of how long I intended to be out here and instead tried to sleep while I was running. I tried reciting the presidents backwards. Then the vice-presidents. Next I went to state capitals. Then Canadian provinces. Anything to pass the time. While people came and went I steadily churned along, oblivious to most of what was around me except the person noting my mileage each time I passed the mile marker.

I finished my 26th mile just a few minutes slower than I had ever run a marathon. I figured one of two things was going to happen. I was either going to crash and burn, or I was going to have a spectacular day. To say it was the latter would be an understatement. In fact, I actually quit running altogether with 16 minutes left before the 6:30 PM finish. When told I could probably crawl an extra mile to pad my total in those 16 minutes, I said, "Nah. I'm good." At a pace that averaged exactly 8:30 minutes per mile for half a day, I broke the course record by one mile in total, covering eighty-four miles in 12 hours.

All I wanted to do now was sit in front of the fireplace in the nearby cabin, and savor what I had accomplished. I hunkered at a table trying to figure out how I was going to drive my stick shift home.

It was not until a year later as I was sitting on the plane coming home from Tampa that the ramifications of what I had done in Erie meshed with what I had just accomplished to form an idea. If I run at the right pace, maybe I can run a marathon every weekend for one full year.

5

Genesis

With a grand total of six marathons under my belt, and just a few months after nearly deciding that I would never run a fast marathon, I was off. By the time I got home I already had a plan. My first thought was: one marathon per state, to satisfy a desire to visit every state in the Union while also having a reason to go to, say, Nebraska. But I soon realized hundreds of people had done the same thing already and the idea quickly evolved into a once a week extravaganza, wherever I could find a place to run. I needed to find out if there even was a marathon every single week in the next year. Looking back now, I laugh at how uninformed I was. But how was I to know there were literally hundreds upon hundreds of marathons to be run in the United States alone? I still was a novice to the whole world of marathons.

I discovered websites, communities and running clubs dedicated to marathons. I immersed myself in learning more about the marathon running boom in the late 1970s and early 1980s and learned that it was coming back with a vengeance. However, I soon found that in spite of the plethora of marathons out there, there were some weeks during the year where no marathons existed. While some weekends there were 10 or more, others had zilch. But I would cross this bridge when I came to it. I thought I could either simply run a marathon distance on a treadmill or map out some random course using online maps. I shake my head now when I think about these notions. I feel that if you are not running a race against competition, well, you simply are on a 26.2-mile jog, my friend.

Research showed me that marathons do not always stay on the same weekend that they were the previous year. So, I started out with a rough schedule of the marathons I thought about running and starting making phone calls to race directors. If I did not get an answer, I emailed them. Within a few weeks I had a fair number of marathons planned.

I knew the first weekend of the year I would run the Walt Disney Marathon in Orlando, Florida. The second weekend I had planned on running the Rock'n'Roll Marathon in Arizona. It was there, just a few weeks before, I had qualified for Boston for the very first time. I wanted to make it a part of this excursion. Unfortunately, the weekend that it would take place in 2006 left me with no lodging, as my friend and her husband would be out of town that weekend. While small details like this would later on be barely a speed bump, in my initial planning stages I saw it as a setback and a sign that perhaps I should look elsewhere, perhaps closer to home in a state I had not yet run a marathon. My eyes fell on the Legg Mason Funds First Light Marathon.

The race benefited the Mobile, Alabama chapter of L'Arche, an organization I had never heard of but was curious about. I soon learned that L'Arche is an international, faith-based federation of communities in which people with a mental handicap and those who help them can live, work, and share their lives together. Intrigued, I dropped the race director an email.

A few days later I ran one of the toughest races I have ever entered, the Delaware Trail Marathon. The next day, for reasons that could have been linked to my sheer exhaustion or perhaps because I drank out of the creek on one of the crossings (people shudder when I tell them this; growing up in Northwestern Pennsylvania, I drank out of creeks all the time!) I became violently ill. I called off from work the next day and slept in. When my phone rang I was annoyed that I had not turned the ringer off but answered it anyway.

The phone call was from the race director of the First Light Marathon and the director of the Mobile chapter of L'Arche, Marty O'Malley.

6

L' Arche

I told Marty of my plan and we talked about how I could help L'Arche. By the time the conversation was over, I knew I had a purpose higher than my own. Through running I hoped to not only raise awareness, but also $52,000 for L'Arche Mobile, $1000 per marathon. I had worked in the past with mentally and physically handicapped persons, and had good friends who had family members who were also challenged; this organization spoke in a special way to me. The mentally and physically handicapped are often the overlooked people of the world. I knew every cent I raised would help L'Arche and, more important, the awareness I would raise for a relatively unknown organization would far exceed that monetary amount.

I had a direction. There was much to plan, so many more marathons to look at, so many, many people to convince to become sponsors (and so many, many "no, thank yous" in response) but. I spent the next several months getting to know more about L'Arche Mobile and L'Arche as a whole.

Welcoming people from many different faith traditions, as well as people who have no formal affiliation with any particular faith tradition, L'Arche communities typically include homes and day programs.

L'Arche was founded by Canadian Jean Vanier in 1964 when, through his friendship with Father Thomas Philippe, a Dominican priest, Vanier became aware of the plight of thousands of people institutionalized with developmental disabilities. Vanier felt a divine call to help. He invited Raphael Simi and Philippe Seux to leave the institutions where they lived and share with him a real home in Trosly-Breuil, France. He named their home L'Arche, which translates in English to "The Ark."

From this original community in France, 130 other communities have been founded in all parts of the globe: Europe, Africa, Asia, Australia, and North and South America. The first L'Arche community in the United States was founded in 1972 in Erie, Pennsylvania. Today, L'Arche USA has 16 communities and two projects nationwide.

Although L'Arche communities are found in many different cultures and reflect the ethnic and religious composition of the locales in which they exist, they share a common philosophy and approach. The L'Arche Charter says, "In a divided world, L'Arche wants to be a sign of hope. Its communities, founded on covenant relationships between people of differing intellectual capacity, social origin, religion and culture, seek to be signs of unity, faithfulness and reconciliation." The Charter further outlines the objectives, the principles and the identity of L'Arche. All the Communities of the International Federation are committed to living these principles.

It is my one regret, that, with traveling to a different marathon location every weekend of the year, I could not visit L'Arche Mobile as much as I would have liked. While I was only able to meet once with the core members and helpers of L'Arche Mobile throughout the entire year of running, Marty O'Malley's emails helped me feel connected.

However, I soon found a chapter of L'Arche in Washington, D.C. and tried to make it there to get my L'Arche "fix" as often as I possibly could. Eating dinner with the core members and sharing their experiences always left me with a smile. I got to witness firsthand how the core members and the workers lived together and fully experienced their lives as a family. I could see how much they cared for each other. I may have come into the house sore from the last marathon but I left with a renewed bounce in my step. I began to see comparisons between the L'Arche core members and marathon runners. Both possess a certain unwavering will to succeed. Often both parties face almost insurmountable odds. And without a doubt, both inspire others to achieve things they never thought were possible.

I finished the year making small radio appearances, creating Fiddy2 apparel whose proceeds would benefit L'Arche Mobile, and contacting more people, in more random walks of life than you can possibly imagine. It made me a stronger person and a more patient person. I learned to deal with disappointment and also learned how to temper my excitement. Never too low or high I took all news in stride because I had to do so. No matter what happened, six or seven days later I would be running another marathon.

I ran a few more races, setting a personal best at the Marine Corps Marathon and then tackling a 50 miler a few weeks later, all to build up my body for the year to come. Just a few days before the end of the year, I met a girl through a mutual acquaintance who would become my best friend, biggest supporter of Fiddy2, and my publicist. You will hear about Anne through the remaining pages of this book and for good reason. Without her, I would have never accomplished what I did in 2006. Fiddy2 was more or less a one-man show as I coordinated my travel, hotels, car rentals, race fees, and everything else that goes into traveling to and running fifty-two marathons. However, it is no secret to anyone how integral to this process she was and how lucky I was to find her when I did.

The remainder of this book is a race-by-race recap of my year. In similar posted weekly recaps on my website, I actually earned the gratitude of race directors who were pleased to see someone give an honest review of their race. By the time the year came to a close, I actually had race directors grab me at the end of race and say: "Even though you are always truthful, I know you hold back in your recaps. But right now you are too tired to use any filter. How did it go?"

Thumb through the rest of this book; pick and choose the races that interest you, and know that you will get one runner's perspective on everything involved with that race. I hope the information serves you well.

If what I have to share also inspires, then my job is done.

7

The First Marathon of Fiddy2

Marathon 1
Race: Walt Disney World Marathon (and Half-marathon), Orlando, FL
Miles from home: 851.1
26.2 miles raced
1336.2 miles to go

Finishing Time: 3:48:18
Place: 1182nd

As the New Year started, there was no shortage of disbelievers in my quest. Honestly, who could blame them? Not many people have run 52 real marathons in one year and I could find no record of anyone doing them as fast as I was planning on running them (all under four hours). Throw in the fact that of my 12 lifetime marathons, 8 had been run in the previous year, and there were many reasons to doubt me. So, I decided to thumb my nose at everyone and no one in particular and signed up for the Goofy Challenge.

Of course the highlight of these races is running through the parks, however, the majority of the course is on access roads or through parking lots. When you do run through the parks it is often a little difficult, as the areas cordoned off for runners are not nearly as wide as the available running space. Lots of sharp turns as you weave through the Magic Kingdom can leave the ankles sore.

Furthermore, the two toughest parts of the course are ones you will never hear about from the race organizers. First is where runners trot behind what appears to be the waste treatment plant for the entire facility (one runner with me during the half-marathon exclaimed: "Is that the Happiest Septic Tank on Earth?"). Second, around mile 21 or 22, you are taken down about a mile of highway with no scenery and fewer crowds. Worse, you have to turn 180 degrees and run right back from where you have just come. Hordes of people streaming back at you, when you cannot see exactly where they made the turn-around, especially this late in the race, is demoralizing.

Still, I was extremely excited to put the planning behind me and actually start running, beginning with the half-marathon. I knew the course and what to expect. One thing I did not expect, however, was the 30-degree Fahrenheit temperature on the morning of the race.

I wanted to make sure that nothing went wrong on this first race of the year. I caught the earliest bus to the starting line. As I stood around at 4:50 am, I realized I was severely underdressed in a singlet and shorts. Oh yeah, and big Mickey gloves. Damn it, I was determined to have fun this year. Luckily for me on this freezing morning, the gloves helped keep me warm as I continually rubbed my body down. Someone finally felt sorry for me and gave me a garbage bag to throw over my shoulders. Unless I am mistaken, it was none other than John Bingham, aka The Penguin. Bingham is a well-known runner/writer who stresses the enjoyment of racing and signs all of his articles with the phrase "Waddle on, friends." I knew little about the lore of marathons, the famous names in running or the rich history of the sport. So, when I say I think it was John, it is only because it could have been some other chap who was lucky enough to be up in the "elite" corral where I was stationed.

Why was I there? To their credit, the Disney people were absolutely wonderful to me, graciously accommodating someone who had not actually accomplished anything yet. As the year rolled on, and it became quite clear it would take a train wreck to stop me from accomplishing my goal, few others were as giving as Disney. This gesture, at the very beginning of my entire year, became even more appreciated when it was seldom repeated. I am extremely grateful for it.

Nevertheless, the half marathon started and a rather unremarkable race went by for me on the course I described above. No matter, I have lots of shots of me "high-fouring" fans in my Mickey gloves. When I crossed the line in 1:38:42, I was just so pleased to have begun the year. And now I was ready for my real challenge to begin. I could write a book on all the people I met in this marathon alone, from the gentleman running in memory of his 4-year old daughter who had died of a brain tumor, to the older gentleman running for our troops carrying a flag in each hand. I can see why it is nice to not "race" a race once in a while. But two moments left an indelible impression on this first of 52 marathons: its beginning and its end.

Picture, if you will, a runner who has been planning to run 52 marathons in one year. Now, imagine him praying that whatever might go wrong in one year, it not go wrong enough to prevent him completing his goal. Picture him at the beginning of the very first marathon of this quest. It is pitch black because of the early morning start time. He has listened intently to the Star Spangled Banner and is virtually seconds from the start. He is excited to finally begin running. His mind wanders for a second. He checks out the nice legs of the girl next to him and notices her ChampionChip (a timing chip worn by runners to calculate their exact running time. Without them, a runner doesn't get credit for a race of this magnitude.) He thinks how invaluable these chips are to racers. He suddenly realizes: HE DID NOT PUT HIS CHIP ON THAT MORNING.

Seconds before Fiddy2 was to finally start I had the nauseating feeling that Marathon 1 of 52 was not going to count. I had already messed up what was going to be a long year by forgetting the simplest of things. Frantically, using all of the contacts I had made in the previous days, my cell phone, my VIP pass and some hurdling skills over barriers that would have made Edwin Moses proud, I solved my problem. I got in touch with the timer of the event, who actually gave me his own personal timing chip and programmed it into the system. I would be counted officially. But I still had to make it back to the starting line.

The gun had long since sounded and runners were now streaming by en masse. I had to cross through all of these runners to get back to the correct side of the highway and then run about a mile back to the timing mat. Only then could I do a u-turn and begin running, seven full minutes after the clock had started. In fact, it wasn't until a few weeks later that my time officially showed up in the results and was counted.

So that is how I started the first marathon of the year. Sheer panic followed by the utmost of joy. The marathon itself was rather uneventful. I hooked up with a fellow Penn Stater and ran a vast majority of the race with her. When one us would fall back or surge forward the other would always catch up. As we neared the end, I pulled out my cell phone. Why? Well, I knew my father (crippled in a hunting accident before I was born) would not be able to see me finish any of the races this year. So I took my cell phone in order to have him "with" me when I finished the first race of the year.

Here is how the phone call went.
(My dad remembers it somewhat differently)

Me: Hey dad!
Dad: Hey. Wait. There's too much background noise. I can barely hear you.
M: I know! I am running among hundreds of screaming people, Dad!
D: I can't hear you. I think it's my cell. Let me get my earpiece. (shuffling)
M: DAD! NO! I have, like, 100 yards to go. Get back on the phone!
D: (more shuffling)
M: DAAAADD!
D: Ah there we go. (pause) Nope. Still bad reception.
M: Dad it is NOT bad reception. It's screaming people!
D: What? Where are you?
M: Running a marathon. Remember the whole big long talk we had about how we love each other but don't really show it all that much and how I wanted you to be with me as I crossed the finish line of my first marathon of 52 in one year?
D: Sorta.
M: Well, I have about 15 feet until I do that!
D: And you are running while on your phone?
M: YES!!!!
D: (pause)
M: Hello?
D: You get this weirdness from your mother's side.

One marathon down.

Kicking off a year of running, Dane calls his Dad at the finishline of the
Walt Disney Marathon.

8

L' Arche Mobile's Marathon

Marathon 2
Race: First Light Marathon, Mobile, AL
Miles from home: 966.2
56.4 miles raced
1310 miles to go

Finishing Time: 3:28:29
Place: 22nd

The First Light Marathon in Mobile Alabama was coordinated by, and benefited, L'Arche Mobile, the organization that was the crux of all of my fundraising efforts. Many of us are charitable with our time and money but rarely do we get to see, first-hand, the actual people we are helping. So, you can imagine how excited I was to finally meet in-person the core members of the L'Arche Mobile community and get a chance to see those who would benefit from my running in 2006. And meeting Marty O'Malley, the race director and director of L'Arche Mobile, after months of emails and phone calls, was a treat. I found that my hotel also served as the small race expo/packet pickup and was very conveniently located about half a block away from the start of the race the next morning.

At the pasta dinner the evening before the race, I spent a great deal of time with many of the core members of the L'Arche Mobile house. With the recipients of whatever I raised sitting around me slurping up spaghetti, I never stopped grinning all night long. Sitting here in Mobile with these folks felt great. It mattered not that, for the most part, the core members knew nothing about the storied history of marathons or even what I was going to be trying to do for them in 2006. What mattered was that someone who cared about them was going to do his best to make their lives better. I can tell you this: I slept soundly that night.

The morning was beautiful. The temperatures were a little cool but the cloudless sky seemed ready to warm Mobile. The previous year's race had been marked by sweltering temperatures. I said a little prayer of thankfulness that there did not appear to be a repeat in the works.

I received a small introduction of sorts over the loudspeaker at the beginning of the race. As I was only one marathon into this quest I received a few looks of "Yeah, right!" from what appeared to be some of the more seasoned marathon veterans. I find it extra invigorating when people doubt what I plan to do; I simply smiled and gave a wave.

There was much anticipation in the air; one of the core members was going to be firing the starting pistol. I'd learned the night before that, in the excitement surrounding race day in the previous year, the core member had fired the pistol prematurely. To prevent a repeat, this year the core member would simply be holding a volunteer's arm and pull down on that arm to allow the starter to fire the pistol. Personally, I liked the idea of an unannounced start better.

The plan to simply finish the marathons in under four hours was still intact. So, when the gun went off I started off far below the pace I normally would run in a marathon. Wearing a GPS on my arm that allowed me to know exactly what pace I was on, I tried to stick to it as closely as possible. While my engine was revving and I wanted to take off, I knew I had 50 more races to do this year. Nevertheless, while talking about my plans to a few runners in the pack around me, I soon found I was running faster than I should. I had to excuse myself and fall back. I met a few other runners, in a slightly slower group, and made even more new friends. I was going to enjoy this "running easier" idea!

As we ran through the tree-lined streets, devastation from Hurricane Katrina was still evident. Mobile had been spared most of the destruction, but you could see signs, some six months later, of the damage that storm had caused.

With more energy than the week before, since I hadn't this time run a half-marathon the day before, I decided to run the first half in a 7:45-minute per mile pace and then the second half in a 8:15-minute mile pace. This would put me right near 3:30 for a marathon time with a little leeway.

I was told there was a pretty bad hill around mile 18 and steadied myself for it. Around the place where it should have been we crested a small rise. I turned to a man on a bike next to me and asked him where the big hill was going to be. He told me I had just conquered it. I laughed out loud. He smiled and told me that to runners in the south that WAS a hill.

For the next few miles this gentleman, who I learned had run this marathon in previous years but had been sidelined with an injury, would ride ahead to assist with volunteering of some sort and then ride back to me to tell me where the aid stations were or where other runners on the course were in relation to me. It was extremely nice of him, and as the sun came out and began to warm us, his information was quite useful.

A few townsfolk came out onto their yards to cheer on the runners in the last few miles before we turned onto a street closed to traffic. Runners traversed through the heart of Mobile, a section that was nothing but old time town shops and locally owned restaurants. Before long I could see the clock ahead and the park behind it with the party already underway. I pushed hard to finish ahead of schedule and ran a 3:28:29, just shy of 20 minutes faster than I had in Disney the week before.

Immediately upon finishing, the greatest finisher's medal out there was placed around my neck. Hand-painted by an individual core member from the L'Arche Mobile home, every medal was unique. In addition, having won my age group, I was presented with my own plaque. Like the medal, this plaque was designed and created by a core member at L'Arche. I wish I knew which members created both so I could give them a big hug. And believe me, if you have been around any L'Arche core members, you know hugs are free and plentiful.

9

Florida Running

Marathon 3
Race: Orlando Xtreme Marathon, Christmas, FL
Miles from home: 856.2
78.6 miles raced
1283.8 miles to go

Finishing Time: 3:40:06
Place: 7th

The first Saturday marathon of Fiddy2 had me running in some of the hottest and most humid conditions I had had the displeasure of encountering so far (oh, how things would change in the future). After the race, the dehydration I suffered lead to some intense cramping in my calf muscles, my thigh muscles and even my pectoral muscle (explain THAT one to me!) A conservative estimate of runners who quit somewhere out there in the Florida swamp equals a solid one-third. (Hopefully none to the gator I saw swimming around one of the ponds like a primordial missile Even in my heat stroke-induced state, sight of this guy made me a tad more alert).

A late start was not the only trouble we would face during the race. At a point during the first of our loops some of the very first runners actually cut the racecourse short by about a quarter of a mile. I was among the first runners to notice the deviation from the correct route and two new friends (Joel and Helen) confirmed my suspicion.

However, in spite of this rather inauspicious beginning, we all felt the flat terrain would make the four-loop course one we would be able to knock out easily, even as the sun began to cut through the morning sky. Before we knew it two laps were down and we were more than half way home. Unfortunately, somewhere in the third lap the relentlessness of the sun's rays made us all feel the strain of the simple left-right, left-right. Helen fell back first and soon Joel followed. When the fourth lap hit, I was running by myself, my two new friends somewhere behind me on the dry trail.

The dusty monotony of running the last 10 miles was far from enjoyable. I was thinking the end would never come and it assuredly did not help that there were dozens of buzzards or vultures circling overhead. When they landed in the crooked dead trees of the abysmal swamp and stared at us menacingly, I wanted to yell, "Runners make bad eating!" I swear they had planned their family reunion for this weekend.

Finally, I stepped across the finish line to the surprised applause of maybe seven people. Given the looks on their faces, I don't think they were expecting anyone! I placed 7th overall and won my age group with a time of 3:40:06 (couldn't be 3:39 could it?) My pre-race goal of a 3:35 had not been met but I was beginning to believe the words I had once heard about a marathon: "If you finish, it is a victory."

Helen almost caught me at the end and was the women's overall winner. Quite a kick she displayed for a muggy-warm day. In addition, and I haven't the foggiest idea where she was stowing it, but right after the race, standing in line to get massages, Helen whipped out a checkbook and made a donation to L'Arche. Amazing!

I was told I would be in the gossip rag In Touch Weekly. Sure enough, at a grocery where I was picking up some Gatorade, I opened to page 79 and there I was in a few pictures and words. I bought my Gatorade and a candy bar and plunked the magazine down on the counter as well. The young clerk raised an eyebrow at my purchase and I pointed to the article. "That's me." She did a double take. "Cool!" I realize it's hard to impress a 16-year-old, so I felt pretty good.

As I climbed into my rental car, I wasn't sure how I was going to do this 48 more times. But I knew the next day, through the grace of God or pasta, I was going to go on a short jog to limber the muscles up and hope to once again be amazed at how good I actually felt. While I have never received a gift horse, I know very well not to look it in the mouth. So no questions as to how or why but only what's next.

Marathon 4
Race: Miami Marathon, Miami, FL
Miles from home: 1061
104.8 miles raced
1257.6 miles to go

Finishing Time: 3:31:30
Place: 262nd

From the start of this race, I knew this marathon was going to be different. Not only was I reconnecting with friends from law school, but I would be helping to pace my former boss (the Honorable John J. Trucilla) to a Boston Qualifying time. Running 13.1 miles with my yammering must have been too much to bear as my judge left me in the dust in the second half. Still, he qualified for the Boston Marathon with time to spare by running almost identical halves of the marathon.

I have no complaints about the Miami Marathon. And as a runner, if you cannot find something to complain about, then that means it was a pretty good day. The race was smoothly run by both the race officials and volunteers; there was plenty of help on the course for the runners; and tons of fluid was made available (essential when you are running in Miami).

The most difficult portions of the course were some of the drawbridges that runners must cross near the beginning of the race and again at the end. The criss-crossed pattern of the open grate underfoot made it easy to turn an ankle. And if a Miami rainstorm passes through this metal can be very slick.

Crowd support was surprisingly little for a race in such a large city but I guess if you factor in the 6 am start time, perhaps not that shocking after all. Sections snake through some nice parts of town such as Coconut Grove and South Beach but for the most part, are not running anywhere near water or beaches. I found this surprising but since open water often means windy conditions I did not mind too much. We did spend too much time in some of the industrial sections of town to please me.

The flat course gave me time to reflect. I was running my fourth marathon in 21 days. After a night to remember with my law school friends I did not expect much performance-wise. So, I was quite pleased with my 3:31 finish.

With one month down, I had averaged approximately 3:35 per marathon, far better than I had expected. I wondered, keeping the bigger goal of finishing the entire year intact, could I try to get just a little faster each week? Was there more in my legs than just barely crossing the finish line week after week in just under four hours?

Maybe I could try something.

Experiment, so to speak.

Marathon 5
Race: Ocala Marathon, Ocala, FL
Miles from home: 807.8
131 miles raced
1231.4 miles to go

Finishing Time: 3:28:39
Place: 20th

Well, apparently I was hydrated enough.

During the first 12 miles of this race, Mother Nature made her call. Six times! I only wish I could have put her on call waiting and run the damn race. I was shocked how often I simply had to pull over to go to the bathroom. However, with my new goal of trying to see if I could get faster each week, I think these little breaks helped eased me in.

It is easy to see why horses are a prominent feature of the Ocala Marathon. Most of the course was through a rolling landscape dotted with horse farms. The hills were part of the course and probably more than most flatlanders would enjoy, but they were not insurmountable. However, given the wind off the open fields the hills seemed more difficult than they normally might.

There were not nearly as many markings as one would hope for in a race that is not intuitively directional. A sparse crowd populated certain parts of the course but often out in the country a runner would be all alone trying to guess exactly where to go. Throw in a few hills at the end where you definitely do not want them; the race could definitely use an overhaul at the finish. Still, I enjoyed myself.

I had agreed to assist a stranger to qualify for Boston and for twenty miles, I thought we had it. Alas, with 10k to go, Bryce, an air traffic controller in Orlando and my running partner for the day, pulled up slightly lame and said: "Dane, I don't have it. Go on ahead." In spite of my coaxing, he insisted this was not his day. I decided that if he couldn't make his Boston time, then I would do it for him. So I gave it all I had to make sure I got that 3:30. After finishing, I grabbed a quick drink and jogged back onto the course. I found him about mile 25 and ran with him to the finish. After crossing the line, he gave me a big hug and said that while he missed his time goal, he was happy nonetheless. So, I wished him good luck and hoped that his reconstructed knee would get him to Boston someday soon. Unfortunately, so far I have found no record that he has.

As for my own race, along with the breaks to make sure Ocala's foliage was properly watered, I did try a new tactic. Having met Bryce early in the race and knowing he wanted to run a 3:30, I decided to give even splits a shot. By doing so, I was able to settle in and keep the same pace. Where in previous weeks I had been nearly exhausted at the end, I found that by running this method I had much more stamina. I figured this might be the best way to approach my races from here on. I also figured I had plenty of races left to find out.

10

Cold Weather;
Good Friends

Marathon 6
Race: Mercedes Marathon, Birmingham, AL
Miles from home: 740.5
157.2 miles raced
1205.2 miles to go

Finishing Time: 3:27:35
Place: 79th

Why must hotels try to get fancy with their showers? Is there anything wrong with just a simple one knob, right-to-left, cold-to-hot, shower fixture? Apparently so, as every hotel I went to in 2006, had some complicated device above the tub faucet that required an engineering degree to use. This week's version looked like the lovechild of a Cuisinart and a breathalyzer. Erno Rubik himself stopped by my room, looked at the apparatus and said: "Good luck." I was actually afraid I might solve the puzzle and open a portal to hell through my bathtub.

The Mercedes Marathon people were kind enough to assist me with lodging. I was paired up to share a room with one of the elite half-marathoners, Chris Wehrman, who ended up taking second place overall for the half-marathon with a time of 1:08 something. This is a pretty darn impressive time, especially given the weather conditions.

Oh yeah. The weather. And the race. Explain to me why marathons always seem to save their biggest damn hill for say, mile 23? And do not get me started on the wind on this day. While not gale-force, the constant blowing took its toll on runners. The 25-degree Fahrenheit temperature at the start of the race only contributed to the windburn my face and upper body received even through a lightweight jacket I wore the entire race.

I once again paired up with a runner just a few miles in who I would share strides with until almost the very end. Katie had decided to run the marathon on a whim simply because she was in town for a friend's wedding. She and I became fast friends during the race and would stay in touch the rest of the year. She is a tiny little runner; I often cut the wind for her during some of the breezier sections of the course. When she offered to return the favor and break the wind for me, I looked at all 5'1", 100 lbs of her and said, "With what?"

We stayed together until the hill I mentioned earlier where I, learning more about my body each week and realizing I run downhill pretty well, opened up a little bit of a lead on Katie. Running fairly even splits once again, I approached the finish with a chance to improve my time from the previous week. I was running alone, into a wind, which had funneled itself through the corridor of buildings and was as strong as it had been anywhere in the race, and time was slipping away.

The previous day I had done an interview with the local news station, and they had filmed me running down towards the finish. I knew exactly how this course would end as it made a twist and then a turn. I quickly ran from the emptiness of early morning streets to a crowded finish area where loads of people braved the cold to cheer on the runners. The announcer saw my bib number and told those in attendance I was on my 6th marathon of the year. This produced a hearty cheer (and in hindsight, I think it is quaint how pleased I was with myself). But at the time, not wanting to disappoint those who were showing their support, I kicked it in and finished in 3:27:25. I had run my fastest time of the year.

Katie finished not much more than a minute behind me. We posed for a few pictures together, exchanged hugs that runners so frequently pass out at the end of 26.2 miles and were assured we would see each other somewhere else on the running circuit. I told her it was easy to find where I would be; just look at the website I had set up for people to track my journey and donate. I never missed a chance to plug L'Arche.

Marathon 7
Race: Washington's Birthday Marathon, Greenbelt, MD
Miles from home: 19.5
183.4 miles raced
1179 miles to go

Finishing Time: 3:30:59
Place: 22nd

When I think about the difficulty of a course I do not often factor in weather. It is so variable that I feel it is unfair to include it in the equation. However, after talking to those who had run this races multiple times, and who said that it is almost exactly the same every year, I had no choice but to factor it into my rating. You see the wind, as it tore across open fields in certain sections, was brutal and relentless, almost standing me up straight at times. I did not envy smaller runners or those not wise enough to use a big lug in front of them as a barrier.

The course starts off on a slight uphill as you wind through the neighborhood of Greenbelt. The wind either stays at your back or is blocked by the trees as you run along slightly winding country roads. Even though it is not closed to traffic, the race leaves you with little to worry about – vehicular movement is light to non-existent. In the summer, I have a feeling this would be a very nice training run. With country air, even though it is just minutes from D.C.'s beltway, and enough hills to keep it interesting you feel like you are miles away from any hustle and bustle.

Through a winding hilly trail you race down a path in the back of people's yards and cross a pink chalked finish line with a cone and a guy with a stopwatch. This is one of the most innocuous finish lines you will find. No problem there. Fanfare is rarely what a lot of us runners are after.

Now, let's play Marathon Jeopardy!

Category: Coldest Marathon in 2006

Answer: He mistakenly thought the Mercedes Marathon would be the coldest marathon he would run in his Fiddy2 quest.

Question: Who is Dane?

Sixty-seven degrees on Thursday before race day gave way to 12 degrees Sunday morning in Greenbelt Maryland. In an ironic twist of fate, I was supposed to be in Austin, Texas that weekend but money concerns kept me close to home in Maryland. What did it do in Austin? Barely got out of the 20s with sleeting ice. I never would have thought Austin would be nearly as bad as Greenbelt in February. Yet in spite of this, the marathon was quite pleasant.

To begin, I spent the first 18 miles running with a new friend. He was wearing a winter hat with horns and a devil's tail, and I immediately recognized him as a runner who had been at the Mercedes Marathon just the week before. I introduced myself. When he told me his name was Rob, I asked him almost without hesitation: "Toonkel?" Sure enough, I had guessed right and realized I just made the acquaintance of a local runner who in 2005 became the 4th youngest person to complete a marathon in all 50 states. So, in three weeks I had met both Rob (who had been following my progress all year and quickly became a good friend) and Wally Herman in Ocala, the first person to ever do all 50 states. It is a small world of marathoning, folks.

As the race went on, Rob and I separated. The last loop became rather difficult as I was running alone and it seemed the wind had picked up. But as I closed in on the finish, I busted serious ass in order to not run another 3:31. My time? 3:30:59.

The cold of the Mercedes Marathon had Dane wearing a jacket during the whole race in February.

11

Wishing Storms
Away

Marathon 8
Race: Bank of America Marathon, Tampa, FL
Miles from home: 909.3
209.6 miles raced
1152.8 miles to go

Finishing Time: 3:26:36
Place: 82nd

Near the end of February, I was hoping the weather gods would stop playing with me!

Awoken at 3:30 am by a thunderous torrential downpour (only 30 minutes before I had to get up anyway, mind you) I knew the marathon was going to be a doozy. Having not yet convinced my brother (whom I was staying with) to actually move into Tampa instead of 40 miles north, I was hoping that Tampa proper might not be experiencing the same rainstorm. Rolling into the self-proclaimed City of Champions, I saw this was not the case as the streets were covered in water. Furthermore, while having slowed, the rain had definitely not stopped.

At 6 am, when the race was supposed to have started, a few thousand of us were stewing very nervously. No announcements had been made but no gun had sounded. Minutes passed. Finally, the loud speaker squawked.

"The race will start at 6:30 am."

Apparently, Tropical Storm ThrowDaneOff had wreaked havoc on police cones, barriers, time clocks, etc.

So, while we bounced around nervously, I decide to do a little Fiddy2 talk to those around me. Believe me, I can throw this topic in anywhere. For example:

"You betcha poverty is a bad thing. Another bad thing: the soreness in my legs after I finish these 52 marathons in 2006 for the Mobile, Alabama chapter of L'Arche in which I am actively collecting donations on my website, www. fiddytwo.org. Funny you should ask!"

Finally, the race started. All those with whom I was speaking planned on running a much slower time, so I decided I might run this one solo. However, just six miles in and I was hurting. The wind was bad. Not horrible but not fun. Rain was ever present, and I was running harder than I wanted to. One of the bad things about running a half marathon at the same time as a full marathon is that runners can get sucked into running with those whose pace is faster than their own. At this point in the year, I had not established my pacing enough to be immune to this pull. So, as a result I had some pains in my side. Then it hit me. I had already stopped once to assist nature in watering the foliage, but I realized my present need was of the sit-down kind. While there were plenty of porta-potties, the first I saw unoccupied was in someone's yard, left over by a construction crew. I prayed it was open and stocked. It was. I soon feel better and was running again.

After that it was an uneventful marathon until mile 22. But I knew what was coming. Having run this in 2005 I knew that as soon as you come out of a little community and hit the bay drive you get sucker punched with a steady head wind.

Headwind: "Oooh, sorry about the fast time you had going there. It is now gone."

Dane (two miles later): "Firetruck you, wind!" (Actually said this out loud. Actually did not use "firetruck.")

I persevered, however, because if my brother was standing out in this mess I couldn't wimp out on him. In the last few miles I passed a baker's dozen of runners and ended up with a 3:26:45. I shouted happily as I crossed the line with my fastest Fiddy2 time to this point. I never thought I would be running this fast!

Could I get faster?

12

The First Races

Marathon 9
Race: Little Rock Marathon, Little Rock, AR
Miles from home: 1011.
235.8 miles raced
1126.6 miles to go

Finishing Time: 3:22:50
Place: 71st

Returning to the course that held my personal best marathon time from March until October of 2005, I was excited to get my World's Largest Finisher's Medal for the second time. Throw in my third marathon of the year with Rob Toonkel, who was kind enough to let me share his hotel room when plans for my own accommodations fell through, and this race had a promising beginning.

This weekend also marked the first time I tried flying in on a Saturday before the marathon, rather than on Friday night. This time, the continual battle to keep the costs of flying down won over my fear that a delayed flight would derail the entire quest. While the time of arrival would be barely more than 12 hours different, if economically feasible, I would not do it again. Being able to get more acclimated to my surroundings and actually be in the marathon city earlier would be my travel plans for the rest of the year, (Ironically, flying out at the crack of dawn on Saturday was barely cheaper than flying out Friday.)

Also for the first time, I predicted a finishing time to my friends. While anything can happen during the course of 26.2 miles, I felt particularly good about this race.

When I forgot my chip for the first race of Fiddy2 the next few weeks of emails from friends always contained the obligatory "Good Luck!! Don't forget your chip!" comments. Whenever running a chip-timed race, I always triple-checked my gear the night before the marathon. As I settled down with my race packet to attach my chip to my shoe I realized I had one little problem.

I had forgotten my shoes.

Those of you who are not runners might not know that a cardinal sin of running is to try new things on race day. The reddest of those cardinal sins would be trying to break in new shoes just a few days before a marathon, especially if they are a brand you have never worn before. I had just purchased a new pair of shoes, so the last thing I was going to do was spend a ton of money on shoes here. I bought the least expensive pair available back at the expo and prayed they would work.

After finding a pair that felt comfortable, I met the local news station for a report to go out that night. It went as smoothly as could be expected and before I knew it I was eating dinner, watching myself on television and falling asleep.

As I stood near the starting line, I scanned the crowd looking for someone I thought would be running close to my pace, so I could talk their ear off. I had not accurately picked that person once. Problem is, unlike me, most people are running the marathon at race pace, and while they may enjoy the conversation, I always feel I may be throwing them off. The problem with playing this little game here was that the race weekend contained a marathon, a half-marathon, and a marathon relay. This meant, unless I specifically stared at someone's bib number and remembered which color meant what, I would not know what race they were running. So I decided to tell anyone who would listen about Flddy2. Some people had heard about what I was doing or had seen my television interview on Fox the previous night.

The course was just as I remembered it. Up and down some smallish hills, the runners went winding through the quaint city streets of downtown Little Rock before circling past the Clinton Presidential Library. After that, a few twists and turns and runners looped back past the start/finish area at the halfway point. Here a nice crowd had gathered, mostly to greet half-marathon finishers.

Unfortunately, passing through this area meant I was about to approach the hardest part of the course: the large hill from miles 15-17. As I climbed the hill, my mind began to wander. It was then that it came to me that the biggest problem with marathons is the unknown. Rarely, when you know what is going to happen, is it ever as bad as you imagined it. (Excluding the bar exam, of course. Don't do it.)

So as I passed through the rest of the race, I was keeping my mind occupied by thinking these thoughts. Around mile 20 or so I passed through the last exchange point for the relay. Soon thereafter, a runner passed me. He was one of the few relay runners who actually attached the word "relay" to his back as was suggested by the race officials. Even though I knew I had run about 21 miles, and he only one, I did not want to let him beat me. So, I began to shadow him. He would gain a few yards on me and then lose a few but I always keep him in striking range. He would pass a runner and then soon after I would. He might as well have had a target on his back.

As we hit the last steep hill at mile 25 (and boy is it steep), I knew he did not stand a chance. I saved my energy as we ascended this final step. I hung back as we weaved through Little Rock. Finally, with that last .2 of a mile in front of me, I pounced. Sprinting by him, and a few other runners, I ran my fastest time of the year: 3:22:50. I was shocked.

In brand new shoes, in my ninth marathon of the year, I was continuing to improve. Wasn't this wrong? It went against everything I had heard about marathons. No matter what the reason, I was happy.

I had told my friends I would run a 3:22.

Marathon 10

Race: Lower Potomac River Marathon, Piney Point, MD
Miles from home: 80.3
262 miles raced
1100.4 miles to go

Finishing Time: 3:22:29
Place: 11th

Let's see:

Have I ever forgotten my chip? Yep!
Left my shoes at home? Yep!
Gotten the wrong race time? Pretty damn close!

I thought this marathon started at 10:30 am. I told everyone it started at 10:30. I had a wake-up call at the hotel for 8:30 am so I could get ready. However, right before going to bed, while searching the marathon website for something completely different, I noticed that the marathon started at 8 am. Thoughts about the ramifications of me moseying into the starting area around 9:55 and realizing I was two hours late shot through my mind. As there was no chip time, I would have had my first 5-hour marathon time ever. I would have had no choice but to simply start running and finish the race.

Luckily, I calmed my semi-heart attack, changed my wake-up call and fell asleep (only after tossing and turning and setting three separate alarms.) I woke up feeling refreshed, mainly because I knew I was going to make it to the race on time. And what a race it was.

During the first few miles I was able to spend some time with a marathon newbie, Nate. Nate did wonderfully well for his first marathon ever even though we both went out way too fast. During our run, I learned he was going to flight school during the summer and this was his last chance to squeeze in a marathon. When I found out later he came in right around 3:40, I was so proud of him.

As my publicist Anne had traveled to the marathon with me and hopped into the jeep of a running friend, I had some nice crowd support up and down the course. Of course, two girls sitting on the roof of a Jeep, sunbathing by the side of the course made many more friends than I did!

As I expected from the description given to me by friends who had run the race previously, the first half of the course was pretty. While it was a little windy at times running right on the water of the Chesapeake Bay, beautiful bay homes, wind-blown beaches and boats sailing in the sun made for a pleasant 13 miles. In fact, if real estate is cheap there, I highly suggest you buy some. Just gorgeous.

Unfortunately, the second half was a straight out-and-back on the highway with cars flying by and the sun beating down. I forgot to mention earlier that it was very warm (close to 80 with a cloudless sky) and I thank my lucky stars the race did not start when I originally thought it would. I remember showering afterwards and seeing my nice singlet tan; and watch tan; and socks tan; and short shorts tan.

What really hurt a great many runners mentally was how the course was mis-marked at the end. When mile 26 showed up, we were definitely much further away than two-tenths of a mile. If you have saved about .2 of a mile's worth of energy, knowing you are even a foot farther away can be demoralizing.

In fact, I think some of the demoralized were the four people I passed in the last half mile or so as I gave everything I had to try and break my previous week's time. With the taste of competition still fresh in my mouth from Little Rock, I could tell I was really beginning to race each week. And in this smaller marathon, I actually had a chance at a top 10 finish. Of course, some people feel that doing well in a small marathon is somehow less by virtue of the low number of participants. But I do not feel the same way.

When I crossed the line, I had truly given all I had on that day. I did not break the top 10 but almost got there with an 11th overall place. I felt no shame that only 129 runners completed the race. I am sure someone has said it far better than me but my feeling is this: One can only race those who show up.

And even though it was not a huge improvement over my time at Little Rock, when I finished my 10th marathon of the year in 3:22:29, I had improved yet again. I was ready for the next challenge.

13

Wearing a Tiara

Marathon 11
Race: Shamrock Marathon, Virginia Beach, VA
Miles from home: 454.3
288.2 miles raced
1074.2 miles to go

Finishing Time: 3:18:41
Place: 138th

Having started my endeavor in January, I knew there were going to be times where I was faced with inclement weather conditions. I thought I had handled those thrown at me so far in the year rather well. But nowhere had I been head-on with constant winds like I was at the Virginia Beach Marathon. From the turn-around heading south at mile six to mile 19, a steady wind constantly threatened to blow off my tiara.

This was the weekend of meeting friends. From the trip down to Virginia Beach with Diana (thanks for driving, I surely did not want to do so on the way home) to meeting a high school buddy (Jason, thanks for standing out there at mile six and somehow making it to the finish) to cheering on fellow running friends (way to go Diana, Mauriella, Jenny, Kacey, Mike, Megan, Christy,

Christa and others) to meeting the wonderful ladies from Girls on The Run who bestowed me with my lovely tiara, I could only wish I had more hours to spend with all of them.

As for the tiara, on this day, I was running not only for L'Arche Mobile but also for an organization called Girls on the Run, an after-school running program for girls in third through eighth grade to help build self esteem. Team Tiara is the charity running leg of Girls on the Run. Team members run in "sporty" tiaras, which show the whimsical spirit that exists within the girls and caps off their image of strong, healthy women who dare to make a difference. I had met some of the Girls on the Run higher-ups at Disney; we had stayed in touch and realized we were both going to be at Shamrock. They asked me to be a member of Team Tiara.

The course started out great, flat and straight and the wind at our backs. Maybe that's why I clocked my first mile in the 6:30s. Whoops! It was here, when the 3:10 pace group passed me from behind, that I realized I needed to slow down (my average mile pace for my last race had been 7:44.) In the group passing me was a gentleman named Tom who shouted out to those he was leading: "This guy is running 52 marathons this year!" I was as surprised that this guy knew who I was as the people in the 3:10 pace group were that the guy wearing a tiara and running his eleventh marathon in 10 weeks was in front of them. What I learned later was that Tom was on the local administrative board for Girls on the Run and so knew exactly who I was.

Speaking of the tiara: I was given a choice of purple or pink.

I thought, "Is there a manly color for a tiara?" before going with the purple.

It was around mile 3 that the first gust of wind took that tiara straight off my head. Luckily, I had separated myself from the pack and had time to chase it down. I realized I was going to have to attach this thing to my head in a more secure fashion. For maybe the first time in my life I was glad I have ears that stick out. I took the coiled cord, which had simply been going around my head, and hooked it under my ears. The wind blowing the front of the tiara against my forehead stabilized it. I had put together a secure little contraption. All while running.

There were no more tiara incidents the rest of the race.

When Mike Wardian, the eventual winner and member of my own running club, passed by me in the opposite direction, I did not know I was going to be running into a ton of wind real soon. Obviously wind in your face is difficult. But one thing that really started to get to me was the noise. Thirteen miles of this loud "whoosh" in my ears was just about enough to drive me over the edge. Finally, around mile 20, the wind finally went from our faces to our backs as we made the turn back home for the final 10k.

While I was really gunning for my best time of the year, I was not taking myself too seriously. I mean I was wearing a tiara for goodness sake. So when I spotted an exceptionally cute dog at mile 22 or so, I simply came to a stop and knelt down in front of it for a big sloppy kiss. Dogs love marathon runners. (Could it be because of our salty sweat?)

I honestly believe that stopping to pet the dog gave me an unexpected boost as I really began to kick it into high gear. The wind at my back undoubtedly helped, as did the boost of running past hordes of people going the opposite direction. I cruised down the boardwalk next to the ocean and focused on the big Neptune statue, which represented the finish, in the distance.

Tiara plastered to my head, I ran my fastest time yet in Fiddy2 and this marked the seventh race in the last eighth where I bettered the previous week's time.

This venture had definitely reached the point of being fun.

As a member of Team Tiara, Dane supports Girls on the Run, an organization dedicated to keeping young girls fit nationwide, at the Shamrock Marathon.

14

WinningTwo Bets

Marathon 12
Race: National Marathon, Washington, DC
Miles from home: 9
314.4 miles raced
1048 miles to go

Finishing Time: 3:16:31
Place: 56th

Every sign pointed to this being one of the first marathons in awhile where I did not lower my time from the preceding week. Some of these things I knew up front and some I did not.

Upfront:

I had been feeling under the weather since Wednesday.

I had a short week of recovery, as this was a Saturday marathon.

It was my twelfth marathon of the year, or the exact number I had run over the previous five years. And contrary to what I was continually told, no, the body was not getting "used to it".

Learned on the course:

After the nice quick run through downtown DC, miles 13-20 were much more hilly than expected.

And after mile 20, the hills became downright nasty.

Running along stopped traffic for three miles means you get to breathe in the fumes of hundreds of parked cars.

Which brings me to my little spiel on the inaugural National Marathon. In spite of the gloom and doom about this race, it ended up being okay. I say okay because it was not great. Granted, not every marathon needs to be as flat as a pancake but six separate steep up and down hills in the last 10k, alongside stopped traffic is undesirable. (For the 2007 race, a changed course had none of those hills)

Still, there were pleasant surprises as well, especially a section of DC called Anacostia, a neighborhood in DC that is...ahem...not so upper class. We joked during the race about where we could buy lightweight, wicking bullet-proof vests for the miles. But here's the thing: the people who came out in Anacostia were just great. Random people going about their early morning day, or going to church, or what have you who probably had no idea what in the hell was going on were all very supportive. This is something I hope gets recognized.

I carpooled to the start with Rob Toonkel, who was running this marathon and then another one the next day (because, in his own words, "I have to do something to one up you!" I love friendly competition.)

At mile 12 I saw my friend Mike with whom I had run the Marine Corps Marathon in 2004 but had not seen since. We stayed together until mile 22 or so when he finally pulled away from me and finished very impressively. I am now 0-2 against him. Jerk. (He did say my form had changed a great deal for the better since late 2004. My rebuttal: "That was my third marathon. This is my 24th. I sure as hell hope so!")

59

The last few miles, as I said, were difficult. I had heard about the hills at the end but was hoping they were not too bad. Unfortunately, topping each crest revealed just another one on the horizon. When they finally flattened out I could see a stadium in the distance, signifying the end of the course and it was a most welcome sight.

I was starting to fade. With just .2 of a mile to go, I saw a sizable crowd had gathered to cheer everyone on. That's when I heard, courtesy of Anne, something like: "...and coming in wearing the electric blue jersey is Dane Rauschenberg. Dane is running his twelfth marathon this year to raise money for L'Arche Mobile!" Anne had gotten the ear of the announcer, camera crews and I think possibly introduced herself to the 200 or so people in the finish line. My last 90 seconds of running was accompanied by some wonderful cheers.

I had bet Anne I would set another Fiddy2 PR. I won the bet with a 3:16:31. On a side note: I was home, showered and ready for the day by noon on a Saturday. That was pretty nice.

Marathon 13
Race: Glass City Marathon, Toledo, OH
Miles from home: 470.8
340.6 miles raced
1021.8 miles to go

Finishing Time: 3:25:45
Place: 46th

In Toledo, I found it more difficult to run much slower than you are able to do than giving all you have.

First, let me say Toledo is a very nice town. I was pleasantly surprised by its relative cleanliness, fine minor league baseball stadium (home of the Toledo Mudhens), excellent use of its riverfront property and, not least of all, its well-run marathon.

The Glass City Marathon honors the memory of Sy Mah, one of Toledo's greatest running enthusiasts who once held the Guinness World record for running 524 marathons in his lifetime. On a mostly flat course, this marathon is definitely one where you could set a personal best. Well, as long as the walleye are not spawning.

What?

Allow me to explain. On a four-mile out-and-back section from miles 12 to 16, literally hundreds of fishermen and their monster trucks crammed the narrow road we were running on. Standing almost shoulder-to-shoulder along the Maumee River, these fisherpersons (both men and women) were trying their hand at reeling in some fish. This led to some serious congestion, as hundreds of runners tried to traverse the same stretch of road. This left your not-so-patient author to scream that perhaps the kind gentleman from the Buckeye State may wish to maneuver his unnecessarily enormous "compensator" to another spot on the road that was a lot less head-on-collision-and-vehicular-homicide-esque and more not-being-a-gigantic-boil-on-a-donkey's-hindquarters The fish were not going anywhere and we could be all out of their way in juuust a few minutes. I think I may have been less polite than that.

However, this up-and-down-the-river marathon was actually an enjoyable experience. My good friend Jen from law school was able to traverse the majority of the course, stopping many times to shout out: "Go Fiddy2!" and provide me with great inspiration. Because of her enthusiasm, it was not long before strangers began following suit most undoubtedly doing so without any idea of what they were shouting. In addition, I was running my fifth marathon of the year with Rob Toonkel who was able to hold me off until mile 22 instead of the customary mile 18. ("You are breaking the rules!" Rob declared.) Rob finished in an extremely strong 3:30, even though he had run two marathons in the weekend just prior.

Speaking about Rob's time brings me to my main point. I had made the decision before the race that I was going to run a 3:25 marathon. As I had been getting faster almost every weekend, I decided that I needed to slow down just to make sure I could last for the whole year. The only way I could force myself to do this was to create a new goal. That goal was to run exactly a 3:25.

So the race began with that rationale in mind and until that point in my life there had been few marathons more difficult. Trying to nail an exact minute time over 26.2 miles of running is no easy task when you are, for the most part, still a novice at running marathons. In 12,300 seconds of running (the equivalent of three hours and 25 minutes) I only had 60 seconds of leeway. At the time, I was still wearing a GPS on my arm that assisted in keeping my pace. However, it was far from foolproof for various reasons (some of which are why I stopped wearing one).

Thinking I was right on track, I sauntered along. However, around mile 22, I realized I had made some serious miscalculations. In order to make my predicted time I was going to have to haul serious ass. I began to pass people in bulk along the final miles, and could only hope to make up the difference in the end. As I hit the final stretch, I found out that Jen had spoken to the announcer at the finish line, and for the second time in as many weeks, I received quite a pleasant cheer. I made my goal but sure did cut it close with a time of 3:25:45.

I also decided to never do that again.

15

Rain Then Heat

Marathon 14
Race: Ocean City Marathon, Ocean City
Miles from home: 153
366.8 miles raced
995.6 miles to go

Finishing Time: 3:18:53
Place: 11th

Well, let's get the disappointments out of the way first:

I doubled up on a time I have already run (which went against my goal of knocking out every minute between 3:00 and 3:30.)

I got passed in the last .25 mile of the race.

By being passed, I got knocked out of the top 10 male finishers.

For the third time in as many weeks, I was able to hear the announcer shout my name at the finish and incredulously add, "...making this his fourteenth marathon of the year!" This time I owed the exposure to my friend Sara who accompanied me on the short drive across the state of Maryland. Her un-bridled enthusiasm supported not only me but also a slew of other runners; her cheers and this announcement helped pull me through the ending of what turned out to be a difficult race.

The course is extremely flat. Discounting the only hill on the course (a bridge which takes you out to, and then brings you back from, Assateague Island) this was more or less a track meet. I feel that constant use of exactly the same muscles stresses a runner's body. Moreover, at one rather important place, the course was mismarked.

The last mile marker at 25 was not in the right place. In addition, there were some areas that were being developed for housing where runners could not tell which way they were turning until the last second. Even though I never slowed my pace, that little bit of hesitation as to where exactly I was turning played with my mind.

The aid stations and volunteers did an excellent job of both cheering and providing nourishment, but there were long stretches where I saw no other runner and had no one beside me or in front of me. I found it difficult to keep up a steady pace when there was none I could pace with.

Overall, this race had a very small town feel to it and was excellently run with friendly people at every turn. I knew it was going to be a good weekend when on my way in late Friday night. A sign advertising a pig roast (I think) said we should all go to "Pork in the Park." Throw in the hand-written mud flap on the truck in the parking lot that said, "Be a Flurt (sic.) Lift up your shirt" and I began to think there are some naughty people in Ocean City.

Special kudos to the race directors who contacted me the week before the race to note that I had listed their marathon on my website schedule as being on Sunday, not Saturday, thus helping me avoid another potential disaster (let's count them shall we? Forgot timing chip; forgot shoes; forgot race time, and now forgot race day.)

Pacing my new friend Jeanette (another local runner and mother of three) to a third place finish in the women's marathon kept me going at a good clip. However, when she pulled off to the finish, as I mentioned, I was run-ning alone. The announcer's voice did give me a little spurt and I crossed the finish in a 3:18:53. This was good enough for twelfth overall and first in my age group.

After this race I had fewer than 1,000 miles of racing to go, which was a nice little milestone. I felt nothing was going to stop me.

Marathon 15
Race: Charlottesville Marathon, Charlottesville, VA
Miles from home: 114.8
393 miles raced
969.4 miles to go

Finishing Time: 3:31:49
Place: 27th

Flashback to the Friday night before the race in Charlottesville. I am sitting on my friends' porch in the country outside of town answering emails on my laptop. I have a Jack Russell Terrier chilling on my lap while I wait for my friends to come home. A last-second decision to check out Monticello beforehand had turned out spectacularly when the sky, after a day of rain, turned crystal blue. I was in a great mood.

Jump to the morning of the marathon. After an evening of vicious thunderstorms, the morning broke clean and clear. And warm. And humid. Damn.

The overall course was shaped like a lasso. Approximately 8 miles out on a straight run, approximately 10 miles on the loop and then 8 miles back home.

I had three problems in this first 8 miles:

I was already tired when I finished this first third.
The run was mostly downhill which I love. However, I realized that meant the entire last eight miles was going to be uphill.

I was already sweating bullets, a major problem for me.

When course directors say a course is beautiful I wonder if they realize that runners really do not care very much. As long as we are not running next to a chemical dump, we do not care too much either way. When you are huffing along in the middle of 26 miles, not becoming part of the scenery is far more important than the scenery itself.

I was still on a pace for a desired 3:14 but I hadn't used the bathroom once, and I was still sweating like it was my job. I was ready for the crash.

I held out until mile 18. A gel pack provided a little bit of energy. I realized a 3:14 was out of reach, but a 3:17 wasn't. But slowly and surely, the combination of the warm temperatures, constant hills and rapidly depleting energy stores took their toll. The miles started to go by but so did my time goals.

(I would like to say the water stops went by too but an absolute dearth of them from miles 19.5 to 23 had me shaking my head in amazement. Since most races are put together by former runners, I am always surprised when basic race logistics get messed up. Even if there is no blistering heat like there was on this day, having water at the end of the race is a necessity. Sure, it will not be a magical elixir that saves you when you are bonking but water in the last 10k, at every mile, is absolutely imperative. But I digress.)

Shortly after the 24-mile mark a bunch of kids at a water station started jumping up and down. I figured they were just enthusiastic, and then I heard, "This is the 52 marathons guy!" In the paper handed out to all runners, as well as that morning's local paper, there had been a feature on Fiddy2. Apparently, these kids had read it and recognized me. Honestly, their cheering alone carried me for about half a mile. Then I wanted to pass out.

The home stretch took you through a market area that is blocked off to traffic at all times and is just the epitome of a college town. People sitting outside in the cafes or having ice cream were cheering in throngs as you literally ran inches from where they sat.

(The race had set up cones with big signs stating MARATHON IN PROGESS: STAY CLEAR. Too bad some lady felt that she needed to walk her teacup poodle right at me in this segmented area, oblivious to the fact that I was barreling down at her. At the last second she moved, which was good for both of us as I had neither the energy to go around her, or the energy to pick myself up when what would have been a rather cataclysmic collision set us both sprawling onto the bricks.)

In addition, near the end I spotted my PR chick Anne wearing a "Dane's my Homeboy" t-shirt. She had surprised me earlier that morning by making the drive from D.C. to root for me and bringing her sister's dog, Madison. When Anne saw me she cheered and called, "Are you okay?

I gave a one-word answer, "No."

Damn near stumbling to the finish, I knew I was not going to meet any of my goals except the only true one a marathoner has: to finish. I saw the clock, and I was damned if I was going to run a 3:32. A near-sprint, which almost cost me my vision, pulled me in at a 3:31:55. Almost immediately, an EMT grabbed me. I apparently looked that bad. They wanted to put an IV in me but lying down sent severe cramps up and down my body. I just continued to drink fluids long after saturation point. (Interestingly, although I drank 64 ounces of fluid, at least, and I don't remember going to the bathroom until many hours later.)

But soon, I was feeling fine and happy to know I could handle just about the worst conditions out there.

16

Getting Lost

Marathon 16
Race: French Lick to West Baden Marathon, French Lick, IN
Miles from home: 663.5
419.2 miles raced
943.2 miles to go

Finishing Time: 3:18:16
Place: 7th

High hopes were brought to earth a little bit this weekend. And thank goodness the trip itself was a hoot because the marathon...well...not so much.

Anne had relatives in Louisville, which meant free lodging. But no sooner had we settled into our airplane seats than a gentleman overheard us talking and asked when the marathon was.

"I live in Louisville," he said. "I'm running the half marathon, but I wasn't aware it was this weekend. I've been so swamped at work. Are you doing the mini or the full 24 miles?"

Twenty-four miles? Now my thoughts of him being an avid runner who happened to forget a race were thrown out the window. And what followed was surreal. The man proceeded to pepper us non-stop with questions and fac-toids about marathoning.

"Ever run that Virginia/DC marathon?"

I said, "If you mean Marine Corps, yes I have."

"Heard about the bottleneck they had in Chicago last year?"

"Yes, I did."

"You going to do any running when you're in Louisville?"

"Um...yes."

After landing, the gentleman left the plane before us. The couple in the row turned and said, "Darn, too bad he's gone. We wanted to hear about the bottleneck in Chicago again."

The next day quite by coincidence we actually saw the gentleman out for a run. We crossed to the other side of the street.

In Louisville, I got to experience Thunder over Louisville (a thunderous fire-works display), the official kick-off of the Kentucky Derby. I was able to see the famed Twin Spires of Churchill Downs, ate lunch at Lynn's Paradise Cafe and got to track down the wandering packet pick-up expo. It was supposed to be at a Senior Citizens center that was closed (seemingly for good) when we got there. I noticed a small flyer on the door stating the expo had been moved to the St. Somethingorother Church...with no address listed. No one nearby seemed to know where this church was. I went to a firehall and got the location from the friendly firefighters.

In spite of the precise starting point stated on the website (Start Line is lo-cated "on Red Quarry Rd (25). 98.7 feet from the water drain at the south corner of Red Quarry Rd. and State Rd. 56") and finishing point (Finish line is located" ... at the first stop sign upon entering the school 7 feet from the south curb and parallel to the manhole at the cross section"), the rest of the course left much to be desired, in no way resembling what we were able to discern from the map on the website or any directions given to us. I knew I was in for an adventure.

The day before the race I gave the overall runner list a look-see, and after doing some research, saw I had a good chance to place in this race. A few miles into the race, however, I became aware that people had either showed up who were not on the list, were going to die because they went out too fast, or I was not going to finish in the top three.

The first thirteen miles, while relatively flat, were marked with a genuine ambiguity. The map and directions provided had been more guidelines or suggestions of what may or may not occur rather than actual directions. This "Okay, where do I turn now?" mindset really wears on you. Nevertheless, I felt good; the temperature was much cooler than it had been the previous week in Charlottesville. There was a fair amount of shade and I had a wonderful support team driving next to me for most of the race lending a hand, giving a towel or jumping out of the woods like ninja (Seriously. Don't ask.)

Mile 24 put me pretty close to the finish line. Suddenly, all the markings on the road were gone; any signs with the word "Marathon" and an arrow were nowhere to be seen. Here I was, about a mile from finishing, standing where I knew I should not be. I turned right at an intersection and start running. Upon seeing the site of the meandering expo/pasta dinner, I knew I was north of the finish line. I turned south again and start running back. Now I had no idea where to go. I stopped. I made a right turn and realized I was at the start (not finish line). I started to run back the way I had come. I saw nothing and no one. I turned back around and started to run what is essentially the second mile of the course, frantically looking for someone or something to clue me in. Finally I spotted a guy wearing a medal and recognized him as one of the leaders.

I yelled, "Where is the friggin finish line?" He pointed the one direction I had yet to traverse.

I took off, desperate to find this finish line, and saw where I had made the wrong turn. But instead of having someone at this turn, the volunteers were 200 yards past the turn. I had not seen them and they had not seen me. By now I had to have run 27 miles at least. I looped around, turned a corner, heard some applause and saw a banner. I finished, took my medal and walked away fuming. I voiced my displeasure, came back and apologized for said voicing (profanity-free but definitely irritated) and waited to get my time and place.

I told a few people about Fiddy?, and hopped into my waiting transport.

I felt I had experienced just about everything. And it was only April.

17

Pacing

Marathon 17
Race: Frederick Marathon, Frederick, MD
Miles from home: 47.3
445.4 miles raced
917 miles to go

Finishing Time: 3:19:57
Place: 58th

The Frederick Marathon course is not easy. It is most assuredly not hard either. Rolling hills often appear after long stretches of straight, flat, running where the opportunity to work some different muscles is welcome. It has always been my opinion that an entirely flat course does not lend itself to being the fastest. By continuing to use the same muscles with no deviation, it does not take a PhD. to figure out those muscles will get extremely tired, while others, which are not used, could provide relief. So the rolling hills of this race are exactly what the doctor ordered.

Obviously, the biggest goal of the year was for me was to raise money for L'Arche Mobile. However, even that grand desire can be lost at mile 23 of a hard race. So I was always creating a multitude of goals to keep me interested when the races might get tough or perhaps I got tired. Already I had tried to help people set personal records or qualify for Boston or other time-related goals. Because I was not running at full-speed I had that little extra energy they might not have had.

However, this marathon marked the first time I was an official pacer and got the honor of being the 3:20 pace leader. And kudos to Frederick Marathon. This is how a race should be organized. First, the race started on time. The great course was well marked and well staffed (race volunteers' shirts read "Obey Me"). People were friendly; police officers polite, and there was nary a car horn honked in anger. Finally, every mile for the last five or six there was a fluid station.

With my neon orange "Pace Leader" singlet, I was easy to find. I did not have a specific number to put on my back (there was no planned 3:20 group leader until I showed up) but with a little magic marker at the boor tent and the help of my good friend Kathy, soon my improvised "3:20" marking let all know who I was.

Still early in the race I had a sizable group of people following me like I was the pied piper. I swapped stories, got names and was having a blast. As mile 12 approached I informed all of my runners of my need to use the facilities and dashed ahead of the water stop to use the bathroom. I figured with my patented Quik-Pee system, I would be out before half of them finished drinking at the water stop.

However, when I came out, I couldn't see any of them. I started running again but my large group was gone. I would find out later why.

At mile 21 I caught up to Rob Toonkel and began running with a chap who had never run under 3:34 before. I told him to stick with me and I would get him a 3:20. We then passed my friend Prasad who had done a 50—miler, the Boston marathon and was now here all in a span of just a few weeks. We then turned towards home plate. That is not a metaphor; at the Frederick Marathon you finish inside the Frederick Keys minor league baseball stadium right down the first base line.

I turned the corner and thought perhaps I was going a little too fast. I was right.

However, as my group had either fallen behind me or sprinted way ahead it did not matter too much. You see, I thought we might need to run all the way around the outfield and then come down the third base line. But as we entered the stadium, I found out we only needed to turn left and head down the first base line. With less than 100 yards to go I was staring at 3:19:25. I wanted 3:20 on the nose. So I started walking. One guy passed me. I turned to the crowd sitting in the stands, pointed towards my 3:20 time on my back and pressed them to cheer. They responded. (I think the hotdogs and beer helped). Another guy came up from behind me and I cheered him on as he finished. I then stretched my leg forward, leaned back to look at the clock one last time, and stepped on the mat.

Finish time: 3:20:00.9

It was then that the Race Director who I had become quite friendly with came to me and said. "Way to go on pacing. Too bad your chip time says 3:19:57." As we shared a laugh over my theatrics, three separate chaps told me that they had qualified for Boston and could have never done it if not for me lead-ing the way.

What has two thumbs and loved hearing that? *This* guy!

"You have to have fun, or it is a long 26.2 miles," Dane says.

18

Getting Faster

Marathon 18

Race: Potomac River Marathon, Alexandria, VA

Miles from home: 10

471.6 miles raced

890.8 miles to go

Finishing Time: 3:14:39

Place: 5th

In the first marathon of my fifth month of Fiddy2, with only three more races until I joined a more difficult age group, I stayed local for one last weekend. I realized I would not spend a Saturday night in my bed again until Halloween. Dear Lord.

Starting in a grass field, with a whistle instead of a pistol, the Third Annual Potomac River Run Marathon has come a great way in three years. With elite runners from Kenya and Ethiopia, the field was stronger. Two laps of an out and back course over gentle rolling hills made me give this course a six out of ten on the difficulty scale. The hills were not tough but they were constant with very little running on a flat surface. As for enjoyability, it was a beautiful day (absolute perfect temperatures) and most of the course was shaded.

With the out and back format you got to see all the runners quite often and you quickly became kindred spirits.

Of interest to me was the participation of Mark Zupan. One of the stars of the documentary Murderball (chronicling the US Men's Paralympics Rugby team) Zupan and the members of the QuadFather Association were racing to raise funds for wheelchairs for United States quad rugby. When you feel you are tired and your legs hurt, all it takes is passing someone who doesn't have the luxury of using theirs for you to put your pain in perspective. I saw these competitors a few times and gave them high fives as we passed. Dressed in my all black Washington Running Club singlet, my attire matched their Quad-Father Tees, so I think they considered us to be brethren.

As I approached the turn around for the halfway point I noticed three Kenyans who had been running in a pack as frontrunners had disappeared. It seems they were all having a bad day so decided to quit at the halfway point rather than suffer through. Soon after, I saw someone who had been in front of me earlier, on the ground and receiving medical attention. He was out of the race. While sympathetic, I realized I had a chance at a really high finish in this race if all things went well for me.

The miles went by and I still felt pretty darn good. It was hard to pinpoint exactly what place I was in. Rob Toonkel and my buddy Mike Mills (another WRC runner) gave me updates on the people they passed; I knew I was doing well. But exactly how well none of us knew.

Some miscalculation of the last turn around had me thinking that I was going to come close to a Boston Qualifying time. I was already writing this recap in my head as to how in my 18th marathon of this year I was going to qualify for Boston. However, as the miles to go shrunk from five to three to one, it hit me that my math was way off, that the turnaround point was not at mile 20 bur rather 19.5 and even at a great pace, half a mile is over three minutes.

Nearing the finish line, I came upon a co-worker of mine who had driven more than an hour just to see me race. She was wearing a HUGE Fiddy2 placard with all kinds of pictures of me as well as articles about Fiddy2 attached to it. Talk about an energy boost!

Pushing towards the end, I finished in approximately 3:14:39, which was my best Fiddy2 time by nearly two minutes. While I was happy I was really curious about my overall place. I finished fifth.

Don't get me wrong; my highest ever overall finish left me with joy and exuberance. But one thing about running which will get me until the end is that, even when you are happy, you can still be disappointed. Here, I had what I thought might be my best chance to place all year but I had let it slip through my fingers. Later I learned third place was a 3:06. Then I didn't feel so bad. I had never run a 3:06 in my life and most assuredly did not expect to do it this year.

19

42 Kilometers

Marathon 19
Race: Mississauga Marathon, Mississauga, ON
Miles from home: 523
497.8 miles raced
864.6 miles to go

Finishing Time: 3:16:39
Place: 103rd

Man, I wish Air Canada flew everywhere! For a little flight from DC to Toronto, I had a cushy seat with plenty of legroom, a TV screen in the headrest on the chair in front of me with a selection of movies and music to choose from (I listened to Mozart while I read Lance Armstrong's book and figured out pace stats for this race) and a clean airline top to bottom. Then, once I arrived at the hotel I checked into a room that, while a tad bit pricier than my usual, was super swank. From the folding Chinese screen door leading to the bathroom to the shower placed so I could see through the all-glass doors to the TV, I was pleased

My weekend in Mississauga began early Saturday morning as I flew in on a 6 am flight. After a trip to the expo to pick up my packet and spread the word about Fiddy2 I went back to my hotel to meet the Toronto Post photographer for a photo shoot to accompany their article on Fiddy2.

I had not been meeting as many people in races lately, perhaps because I was running faster. In addition, time constraints had not allowed me to attend many race dinners. This week, the race dinner was in my hotel. I decided it would be folly to not go down and join in.

I sauntered in and immediately noticed five attractive women sitting alone. I decided to join them. These ladies (Catherine, Melanie, Mary Anne, Maria, and Karen) were all running their first half-marathon. We chatted for a bit, and I of course spoke about Fiddy2 and what I was doing before we were joined by another gentleman (umm, hello! Can't you see I am flirting here?) As luck would have it, this chap was one of the speakers at the dinner, and an avid marathoner. In his inspirational speech he even included a quick phrase about Fiddy2.

Race morning came and was seemingly ideal as an overcast sky and cool temperatures prevailed. However, I did have a problem with the possibility of a great deal of wind as the last few miles were run right alongside Lake Ontario. After a rousing rendition of "Oh Canada", a lovely older woman gave us the countdown for the beginning of the race, fired the pistol and away we went.

Around mile 3 (or where I thought mile 3 would be) I realized there were going to be no mile markers, only those denoting kilometers. So at the 5k mark I turn to a fellow runner, a Canadian, and asked, "There are no mile markers. What's that aboot, eh?" He simply said, "It's probably because most people running this are Canadian."

At no point did he realize I was poking fun at the language. Alas.

I ran the first three miles faster than I ever had before. I was hoping to run my best Fiddy2 time of the year to honor my Mom for Mother's Day, but going out too fast was not going to help me do so. I was only wearing a watch that morning and not my GPS so I was basically guessing at my pace. I decided to simply trust my body and run.

A little after the halfway point (which, in spite of my intention to slow down, I ran in 1:35:02) I saw a HUGE sign in someone's yard. Easily eight feet tall, it looked like someone had stretched a white sheet over some two-by-fours. I smiled thinking about how great it is for some people to have fans out there with signs and bells all cheering them on to the finish. Then I got closer to the sign. I had to do a double and then triple take. In enormous letters were the words:

GO Rauschenberg GO!

The Great Dane!!

I couldn't believe it! I ran a little closer and looked at the people sitting on the porch. I knew nary a soul among them. They all looked at me as I stared at the sign, so I pointed at it as I shouted, "That's ME!"

Instantly one of the guys jumped off the porch, ran down to me, whipped out a disposable camera and asked if I wanted a picture with the sign!

Two not-so-quick pictures later, I took off again as he shouted to me that he would send the photos to the Mississauga paper as soon as he could. I had no idea if the pictures would ever get to me, but sure enough, a few months later, I found them in my mailbox. These are still quite possibly my favorite memorabilia from the year.

With newfound energy I took off again, completely forgetting I was already about three minutes ahead of my intended pace. In one stretch ahead, I saw some of the leaders heading back towards me. But with a big old plant looming nearby with its smokestacks billowing forebodingly, I hardly noticed that a majority of the runners were struggling.

At the turn-around, I found out why. A tailwind that I had not noticed now became a full-force headwind. Ooof! For the next eight or nine miles, the course intermittently takes runners into a full-on gale, the worst coming whenever the race path swings down by Lake Ontario. Beautiful indeed, the tossing lake, with its enormous waves crashing on the shore. Getting pelted with wave spray and wind at mile 20 is not!

After another mile of fighting the wind, I could see that I was not going to be able to set a Fiddy2 PR. So I used my energy instead to get the masses of dead-silent spectators to make some noise. They appeared to not know whether they were allowed to cheer. I pushed through the wind and stepped on the timing mat with a time over 3:16.

Ironically, in a race where I had random people making me signs on the course, I had an ego-check at the finish. The race director grabbed me, threw a Mylar blanket over my shoulder and directed me towards a camera crew. The following exchange occurred:

RD: This is Dane. He is running 52 marathons this year. Would you like to interview him? (RD scurries away to do other things.)

CC: Oh, really. (Barely looking at me.) Yeah, thanks but that's okay. Maybe next time.

I admit that my desire to grab him by his lapels and shake him the way a British au pair shakes a baby was rather strong, as I could not for the life of me figure out which "next time" he was talking aboot. I gathered the remaining shreds of my ego and shuffled away.

Dane even makes time in the middle of the Mississauga Marathon to show his fans he appreciates their support.

20

Looping to a PR

Marathon 20
Race: Delaware Marathon, Wilmington, DE
Miles from home: 111
524 miles raced
838.4 miles to go

Finishing Time: 3:13:52
Place: 22nd

When you check into your hotel, and what appears to be a barbershop quartet convention is in your lobby, you know that regardless of the marathon you run, the weekend is going to be interesting. I was amused when two elderly barbershoppers stepped onto the elevator I was on and proceeded to have the following conversation (in reference to some other singers practicing a song outside):

"Can you believe those guys out there are doing Witchcraft?" the one old codger said.

"Well, I guess it hasn't been done in a while. Maybe it will be good," the other replied.

The first old codger actually let out an-honest-to-God, "Harumph." (I thought that only existed in novels.)

At the pasta dinner later that evening, I threw out Fiddy2 business cards like candy. As I had learned through months of fundraising, non-runners do not seem to be nearly as impressed with the guy running 52 marathons in one year as runners tend to be. Having never attempted a single marathon to begin with, they cannot possibly be expected to understand how difficult 52 consecutive weekly marathons must be.

The best way to get donations for L'Arche Mobile as well as getting others to learn about my undertaking would be to speak to those who would be most likely to care. Therefore, the carb-loading dinners before marathons became the place where I would spend my free time every weekend. Detailing my plans for the rest of the year, I still faced skepticism from runners, even here in May where I had nineteen marathons in the bag in nineteen weeks. In fact, the reactions of runners would often fall into two distinct categories: impressed and curious, or completely indifferent.

The first group was a pleasure to speak to for obvious reasons. More often than not they had undertaken similar goals, and therefore understood what I was currently involved in. They offered advice and words of caution.

I think the reason the second group refused to be impressed (even though a majority of those who acted this way only had a few marathons under their belts) was that, unlike others with more experience, they did not understand what is involved with running this many races and could not comprehend the planning that goes into a task such as this. Moreover, they possessed a quality that all runners have in varying quantities: the sense that no matter what they hear others have accomplished, they feel, with enough time and money, they too could do the same.

I honestly believe this is a great attitude to have and one that I am happy to hold myself. Even if it was slightly frustrating at times to be blown off so quickly by people who asked what I was doing, without this attitude many things in life, including marathon running, would be impossible. We would never be able to toe the line at the local 5k hoping to beat that guy we never beat, if we did not think it was possible. When obtaining a Boston Qualifying time eludes us there would be no reason to lace the shoes up once again and try to grasp it, if that spirit was not deeply imbedded within us.

So I did not get too offended by those who were not impressed. Furthermore, I soon learned that listening to people and their own experiences became far more fun than relaying my own.

One of the runners who I had already seen multiple times in 2006 was a sprightly older chap named Phil Little. From Apopka, Florida, Phil was 64 years young. A member of the 50 State and a DC Club member who routinely churns out 25 respectable marathons a year, Phil has long since stopped being a threat to anyone in the upper ranks of a race. My utmost respect goes out to those who know they are not going to set a personal best anymore but who show up anyway. As he would eventually finish in a time of 4:45, beating out over a quarter of the race participants that day, Phil was every bit a champion. I am sure there were friends in this race whom he was happy to see. I am also sure that when he passed one more person near the finish line, a woman 40 years his junior, that he undoubtedly had enjoyed the thrill of the chase.

Marathons are always full of inspirational stories like these. It is these competitors that I looked forward to seeing every week. They make me proud to be among their ranks.

If you did not know the course by the time you started, you had no surprises left after the first 10k. You see the marathon in 2006 was a four-loop course that was about as flat as you could hope for. There were a few slight inclines and some narrow twists and turns that could be improved (runners would be both coming and going on the same walkway and at times their numbers would cause a bit of gridlock), but overall the course was well designed. Without a doubt, you would be hard pressed to find a better course for spectators. With very little effort, a friend could see you no less than 8 times and provide you with the moral support, or food and drink, you needed.

In addition, it allowed runners the chance to offer encouragement to each other. I saw friends Rob Toonkel (in his 74th career marathon) and Cowboy Jeff Bishton wearing his famous Sun Devil cowboy hat. And as in the case in many races, I quickly became friends with other runners as we routinely either crossed paths or provided each other pacing along the way. There is just something about the camaraderie of 26.2 miles that often leaves grown men hugging at the end. Something about going to hell and back often leaves marathon runners with an unflinching desire to embrace, regardless of who is watching.

Anne offered loads of hoots and hollers every time I went through the finish area and made good use of my new digital camera to take some excellent action shots. Getting the crowd to cheer for me is her specialty. Good thing she has talent in that area because I surely do not. This was my 20th marathon of the year (and therefore a milestone of some sort.) I had designed a little sign to wear on my back that said "My 20th this Year!" However, because of an undersized "this", the sign was often mistaken by those viewing it to imply that this was either my 20th year of running or that I was 20 years old. Good times!

When a local Delaware reporter had asked me how I was able to get mentally prepared for a course that had "so many" loops, I realized, for the first time, that running the same course four times might actually be more mentally challenging than I thought. (Thanks a great deal, Kevin Tiesollnii)

Is a looped course harder than others? As with all things in life, it depends. By knowing the layout in advance, you are able to prepare yourself. You have already traversed every inch of the course in the first six-plus miles, so there are no surprises later on. In a marathon, where mental exhaustion plays a large part in one's ability to properly run, every little bit helps.

With the Delaware marathon, that fourth lap is where it finally begins to wear on your mind. In addition, while not as bad as it could have been, almost no tree cover left the runners exposed to the elements. A clear sky and beautiful sun provided wonderful viewing conditions for those who had ventured out to watch the race. But this gorgeous weather added a degree of difficulty for the runners. And by mile 20, I was feeling its effects.

I had been running with a few gentlemen. Stride for stride we had kept each other company and shared tales. But now with less than 10k to go, I could no longer hang with them. They began to pull away ever so slightly. And as much as I wanted to stay with them I knew I had 32 more marathons to go. I could not put in jeopardy the overall goal. So, I decided to dial it back a little bit and see what I could do by reserving some energy.

I had recently had braces put on my teeth. These braces were still settling in and therefore limited what I could chew. On the course, I grabbed a piece of orange from a volunteer, looked at it and then tossed it away. If I had bitten into it, I would have been picking orange bits out of the metal framework for the next two miles. Before the race, I had realized my usual energy bar was going to be far too chewy for my new mouth contraption. So, not wanting to try a different food and possibly upset my stomach, I opted to go without food for this race. You can only imagine how much I wanted that damn orange.

I have found it interesting how in a marathon you can go from total dejection to elation in just a few steps. While I was still pondering whether I should have at least attempted to eat the orange, I came upon Phil Little, powering through his third lap. A hearty "way to go!" from him as he smacked my back. With this little surge I began to pick up the pace again. I knew I was close to setting a Fiddy2 PR, and would pay for the additional effort spent to get it, but I wanted it.

Around one bend and underneath another bridge and I saw the 26-mile sign. Only .2 to go and the seconds were ticking away. Would I break 3:14? I put down my head and started to power through. A woman asked me if it was my final lap and I nodded. She quickly motioned me towards a finish line I had not seen before. My previous loops had taken me to the left and I could not see an arch of balloons, slightly further away, to the right. I could see the clock in sight: 3:13:35. 3:13:40. 3:13:45.

Suddenly, someone surged past me. Where in the Sam Hill did he come from? I realized he was a relay guy trying his darnedest to pick off one final runner as he finished. However, unbeknownst to him, relayers had to keep going straight where I turned right. If he had not been intent on beating me, he would have heard the volunteer. Instead, he had to backtrack 50 feet and go to the left. Ah, what do I care? He had only run 6 miles!

Anne started yelling as she knew exactly what I was trying to do. She wanted me to break 3:14 as well. As luck and determination would have it, I did it. 3:13:52. I called my parents and filled them in. Only a week late, I gave my mother the Mother's Day present promised: my best time of the year. Since Father's Day would have me running at an elevation of 6,000 feet I told my Dad his gift of a PR might be delayed too.

21

Heat Then Hills

Marathon 21
Race: Buffalo Marathon, Buffalo, NY
Miles from home: 454.3
550.2 miles raced
812.2 miles to go

Finishing Time: 3:29:03
Place: 80th

While many parts of this course left something to be desired there were indeed some nice touches. For example, a cemetery that we ran through was gorgeous and just a wonderful touch added to the run. As we celebrated Memorial Day weekend, running through a cemetery helped us remember all those who have given their lives for this country.

Allow me just a moment to complain. I did not want to run this marathon. The race director had been downright surly to me when I spoke with him about assisting Fiddy2 (Just say no. I am a big boy. I won't cry), the weather called for hot muggy temps, and Buffalo is hardly exotic. And unfortunately, from the start of the weekend, all that could go wrong, did. While there is no pressing need for me to list all the woes, suffice it to say I was eagerly hoping that when the race started, all would right itself.

They say that a true test of a man is how well he handles adversity. My addition is that anyone can run well when all is going right. So with everything not working out, I wanted to really push myself in this race to prove I could rise above difficult circumstances.

After the first mile the frontrunners (including myself) were directed incorrectly (or more accurately, given NO direction) and started to run the wrong way. Luckily, at this juncture, the course was an out and back loop so we just ran the wrong side of the loop. However, these are the kinds of miscues that play on your mind for the remainder of the race. You cannot help but think, when is another turn going to be incorrectly marked? Am I going to end up running twenty-eight miles? Will there be enough water?

I was running angry and realized I need to rein myself in, especially since I could feel the heat starting to get to me. I knew at the halfway point that I was in trouble. The hot and humid weather that had been forecast showed up. As much as I hate hills and wind, I hate heat more. It saps me. Down to the core. And I know it. The only thing I can do is hope that I am running fast enough to finish before I am completely drained and exhausted.

Unfortunately, I didn't run fast enough to beat the heat. As each mile slipped away, so did my time. My goal to run a 3:10 or under was gone. Then 3:15, 3:20, and so forth. I knew I had not run a 3:29 yet this year so while I would like to say that I eased up on purpose to run that 3:29, it would be more accurate to say that I pushed hard enough in the last 1.2 miles to make sure that I kept my time under 3:30.

A silver lining in this dark cloud was that I was able to pass out more Fiddy2 cards, tell people about my cause, meet a few other people running their first marathons and run with some fellow runners whom I had seen numerous times this year but had never met personally.

Furthermore, the spectators and volunteers did the very best they could and I wish there was a way for me to thank them all. From the random people not affiliated with the race who passed out liquids that they purchased themselves, to the volunteers who had to quickly master the art of passing along hundreds of cups of liquid to sprinting, cranky, sweaty, exhausted runners, it really is a pleasure to know that there are people who give so much and receive so little. If you happen to be reading this, thank you.

Finally, while this is hardly the way I wanted to run the last race of my 20s, I learned that I could handle adversity.

If you like math, with this race I was now 40% done with Fiddy?

Marathon 22

Race: Deadwood Michelson Trail Marathon, Deadwood, SD
Miles from home: 1654.4
586.4 miles raced
786 miles to go

Finishing Time: 3:26:59
Place: 17th

When I read on the website that the upcoming marathon is scenic, I felt like paraphrasing Rhett Butler and declaring, "Frankly, Race Director, I don't give a damn." I thought that many runners share the same sentiment; as long as the race does not run next to a sulfur mine, meat rendering plant, skunk farm, we really don't care about the scenery. What we can see during the run rarely makes a tough marathon better and it is always the tough marathon that will sing the praises of the scenery. However, after running this marathon, I now stand corrected. A quick note about Deadwood: this is a unique little town. Nestled close to Sturgis (where the enormous bike rally takes place), filled with casinos and history (including, at multiple times during the day, staged "Wild Bill Hickock" gunfights) and little to no cell phone reception, this is definitely a must-see-in-your-lifetime town.

Wonderful views of mountains cascading into sheer cliffs with creeks reflecting sunshine into the valleys were bountiful. The fact remains, however, that this marathon, while not the most difficult, was definitely not easy.

Why? The first half-marathon was a straight 13.1 miles of a gradual grade uphill. Nonstop. After that, the last half was essentially 13.1 miles of downhill. And you never make up the time in a downhill that you lose in an uphill. So we spent the first half chugging up a hill that, while not brutal, was definitely noticeable (especially when you have run twenty-one marathons in 148 days) and the second half in a controlled fall, with quads screaming from the effort.

Let's just say that this weekend was not the most relaxing of marathon weekends. I have told people often (although they rarely believe me) that the running of the marathons is the easiest part of the week for me. When I am racing, I am not focused on soliciting for donations (although if the opportunity presents itself...) I am not hoping my flight is on time and I am not working. I am out for a long (hopefully fast) run where all that matters is the race. Therefore, when the small part of the week that is enjoyable is compromised for various reasons, it adds some frustration to the overall experience.

On the up side, I finally met a person I had been corresponding with for quite some time: Jerry Dunn. Jerry is the race director of this marathon, a runner of 200 marathon distances in one year, a great source of info for me for Fiddy2 and someone I already considered a friend. Unfortunately, Jerry was busy as all get-out this weekend and while he assisted me as much as he could, I did not get to pick his brain as much as I would have liked.

While I saw no exotic wildlife (was really hoping for a buffalo), I did get to meet and talk to about 10 people during the run and tell them about Fiddy2. They regaled me with their own stories, including a runner who was only 18 years old and had run his first marathon at age 14.

While I eagerly anticipated cresting the 13.1-mile hill to start the slightly steeper descent, I realized that as much as I am a good downhill runner, I had never attempted to run a downhill this long. Also, as happens in marathons, the crowd thinned out after the half and I went from running with the company of a few to running alone for the last 100 minutes.

Occasionally, I would pass a half-marathon walker or grab a power drink off of an aid table. I was battling with one gentleman from mile 18 to mile 23 for some unknown placing, when the weekend (or perhaps the year) finally caught up to me. The last three miles turned into a battle to simply hold on and finish in a respectable time. In the last quarter mile I got passed by three more people and ended up 17th overall. I hate to be passed in the final steps of any race but I knew pushing it here would be pointless. I had thirty more marathons to go.

This marathon occurred just days after my thirtieth birthday and many friends asked me if it felt weird to be thirty. I mostly non-jokingly told them I was more upset about moving into a tougher age bracket. Well, Exhibit A: this marathon. I finished fourth in the 30-34 age group; my time would have netted me a first place finish in the 25-29 age group and a railroad spike as an age group award. It appears these spikes were given because the Michelson Trail (which the marathon ran on) was a railroad at one point of time. It was a cool prize and my old butt missed out on it with a time of 3:26:59.

After the race, I got to my hotel, quickly showered, hopped in the car back to Rapid City, flew to Denver, waited around for a few hours, and flew home to Dulles. Forty-five minutes after I got in my vehicle, I was home. I fed my rabbit, grabbed a shower and passed out face-first for five hours just in time to get up, go to work and prepare for a short week before the next race.

What a life.

Concentration is the key in Dane's last race as a 29 year-old in Buffalo, NY.

22

Fightin' the Feud

Marathon 23
Race: Hatfield & McCoy Trail Marathon, Williamson, WV
Miles from home: 447.2
602.6 miles raced
759.8 miles to go

Finishing time: 3:16:24
Place: 6th

To begin, there was a great deal of traveling this weekend. Williamson, WV was not close enough to any airport to make flying a reality but was just far enough away driving-wise (approx. 7 hours) to make it a formidable hike. I booked lodging late for this marathon and the closest place I could find was a three-bedroom hunting lodge twelve miles away from the starting line in beautiful Matewan, WV. An interesting little town with an enormous Berlin Wall-like structure surrounding it (we later found out Matewan has almost been washed away by the flooding of a nearby river on a few occasions), I soon learned the marathon actually ran into, and then back out of town on the only two "streets" in Matewan. Lodge owner Dr. Garland had promised to be outside cheering when I ran by.

In the style of the movie My Cousin Vinny about 100 feet from my bedroom window were train tracks which allowed a VERY active train to make close encounter passes about 5 or 6 times a night. I woke up at 5:30 am and at about 5:31 the train whistle blasted as it cruised by. I'm guessing this was a friendly wake-up call for the locals to begin...well...whatever the heck it is they do. I promised myself from this point on to remember to check out the proximity of loud mass transporting mechanisms in relation to my lodging.

I am not really sure why this is considered a West Virginia Marathon as 99% of it is run in Kentucky, but I am not one to argue with rifle-toting men dressed in authentic pioneer garb. At least I think it was "garb" and not "the clothes I put on today." After checking in at the lodge, we drove to Williamson to the packet pick-up, which allowed me to see what the first thirteen miles had in store for me. Our trip to Williamson actually was made by crossing into Kentucky, right out of Matewan, driving through Kentucky, then crossing back into West Virginia for one block into the town of Williamson. During this drive I passed the starting point in Goody, Kentucky, which is just outside of South Williamson, which itself is just south of Williamson, WV but located in Kentucky. Follow that? Good.

The trek prepared me for a relatively flat-to-slightly-uphill first six miles followed by a backbreaking mile-long hill that crested slightly after mile 7. Best to know ahead of time.

In Goody the morning of the race, I ran into Jeff Bishton (in what I think was our fourth marathon together this year) who as always was wearing his Sun Devil cowboy hat. He introduced me to a young fellow who has run literally hundreds of marathons. Following these pleasantries, we lined up for a quick prayer, and then the race began with a shotgun start (seriously). We'd been told we were in the largest starting field in Hatfield & McCoy Marathon history. There were eight of us.

No, I am kidding. But with over 300 full marathoners toeing the line, my honorary Hatfield heart swelled. You see the race divides every one of the participants into one of two camps – either a Hatfield or a McCoy. Given the hospitality of the race director (himself an honest to goodness Hatfield) I asked if I could represent his clan.

The first six miles were all just build-up to the monster hill. And as slowly as we ascended this hill on the front side, we found we were going to descend it twice as quickly on the other side. It was like someone took the entire course of Deadwood, squashed it together and placed it all directly on this one hill.

However, after going up and back down Mt. QuadKill, it was smooth sailing for the rest of the first half as a shaded, flat stretch kept the intermittent sun off our shoulders. As warm as it could have been in the hills of Kentucky in June, we were all pleased that some deep woods fog kept the direct sunlight from permeating through and sapping our energy. In addition, I had the company of two gentlemen for a few miles (Dave and Shawn) who I would see many times during the day (well, at least Shawn, as Dave ended up toasting us both in the end). But even better than the two-legged variety of companionship, was the little brown dog that followed me for over 3 miles. Step for step, I could not believe that this dog was keeping pace with me. Finally, just outside of Matewan, I had to reluctantly leave my little companion behind.

True to his word, Dr. Garland was standing outside right before the halfway point to yell the following words of encouragement, "Hey! Go...um...you!"

After a four-block run in West Virginia, we passed through the floodwall surrounding Matewan and headed back into Kentucky. Spectators became sparse, the course turned into a trail, the trees and scenery became rather pretty and I am sure I heard Dueling Banjos. Shawn and I ran the next seven miles within sight of each other just so we know that we were running in the right direction, and so we could tell the sheriff where we had last seen the other's body. At one point, a guy in bib overalls whittling away on a stick looked rather unhappy that I was running on the road in front of his home. But it did help quicken my pace!

At mile 19, I saw my travel companion for the weekend and world's greatest publicist for the first time. The Gatorade Anne had waiting for me was very welcome indeed. The sun had burnt off the early morning fog and it was beginning to get hot. For the next few miles, Anne would drive ahead, and come back to tell me what the course was like. This was greatly appreciated for many reasons. I had heard there was another widow maker of a hill at mile 23 and one of her trips ahead confirmed this. Again, knowing ahead of time that you are not going to be having that much fun makes the hard parts easier. I relayed this information to Shawn and his retort was simple, "If there is another hill like we saw at mile 6, I will be walking it." While not as bad, the hill we came to definitely could put a little hitch in your giddy up.

Somehow, however, I gained some strength from somewhere, tackled it hard knowing the last few miles were straight, and strode those last few miles with relative ease. Anne had raced ahead and again I heard the hearty cheer from a crowd who had been informed that this was my 23rd marathon of the year. I crossed the finish line in 3:16:23, which was good enough for 6th place overall and second in my age group. I received a huge trophy and got to talk with David Hatfield again for a few minutes before Shawn came striding in to more cheers.

Normally, I am on my way to an airport soon after a race but with that not necessary and with a friend still on the course, Anne and I decided to go back and cheer her on. It is rare I get to be a spectator, so I jumped at the chance. We found her and later she told us that our cheering and the liquid we provided really spurred her on. She finished very strong for a hard course and a warm day and continued her quest to run a marathon a month this year.

But the star of the show was neither the winner of the race, me, nor any other human. Rather, it was the little brown dog that had run with me earlier. He had been following one person or another for mile upon mile throughout the race. When my friend told us she was fine to run by herself, we quickly drove to the end of the race, found the race director and let him know about the intrepid little animal. Upon hearing my tale, many others mentioned they had encountered him at one place or another. Collarless and looking rather fresh, he probably ran just as far, if not farther than any of us, as he would run with one runner until they left him behind and then would double back and wait for the next runner. With very little effort, I was able to convince Mr. Hatfield that this little fella not only needed, but deserved a medal if he finished.

No sooner than this had been decided, my four-legged friend appeared down the stretch, trotting alone. He had apparently either picked up the scent of the other runners or had been directed this way by people on the side of the road, but nevertheless he was moving right towards the finish. As the crowd began to cheer, he seemed a little skittish and tentative. At one point he stopped running entirely, so I ran forward, grabbed a plate of food (some sort of "vittles" I am sure) and coaxed him across the finish line.

Flashbulbs went off and before we knew it, the little guy was wearing a finisher's medal. "McCoy" seemed barely winded and happily took a drink of water before sitting down at our feet and calmly watching the rest of the festivities. He was apparently a stray, so we made sure that he got the attention he needed before we packed up our stuff and headed back to West Virginia for some well-deserved showers. Before long I was back on the road and seven hours later fell into the world's most comfortable bed for a night of blissful sleep.

The downhills suit Dane just fine as he takes 6th place overall in the hot and humid Hatfield & McCoy Marathon.

23

Thin Air

Marathon 24
Race: Estes Park Marathon, Estes Park, CO
Miles from home: 1713.4
628.6 miles raced
733.6 miles to go

Finishing Time: 3:36:19
Place: 10th

There are a few things that I knew could make marathons difficult for me: heat, wind, bodies of water (invariably, wind will follow) and hills. You can now add elevation to that list of difficulties. I am unsure of where in this hierarchy elevation falls. This race contained high temps (80s), wind (mostly in my face), scenery which is awe-inspiring (uh-oh), and an elevation chart that I had to search for on the website (double uh-oh).

With an elevation topping out at over 8,000 feet, I knew I was in for a challenge. I have had very little opportunity to run at any elevation in my life. Suggestions given to me about spending a few days in Colorado to acclimate myself would have been helpful if I'd had the option to take the time from work. Unfortunately, that was not an option so I just tried to get a good night's sleep as I knew it would be paramount to any hope of success.

I had looked at prior years' results and had hopes of placing well. However, I tempered these expectations as I realized just as I am running most of my races for the first time, so might others. In addition, as race time neared, a quick survey revealed other guys who had decided to try and place. I found out post-race that the slowish times in 2005 had been mainly due to extremely hot weather, so rather misleading as statistics. After pre-race instructions stating that an elk had recently given birth near the racecourse and we should not make aggressive moves toward it if encountered, the race began.

Looking back, I have come to the conclusion that those who run races like Estes Park, are:
Elite runners;
Runners who live or train at high elevation; or
Runners who only run a few races a year.

I am just regular athlete (not elite), live in D.C. (elevation: nil) and well, to state the obvious, run more than a few races a year. So when a pack of nine high-tailed it out of the parking lot of Estes Park High School, I realized almost immediately I was out-classed. I decided to simply run a smart race and let the cards fall where they might.

The first six miles were mostly uphill leading to the highest point of the race. I switched on and off with a few runners ranging from 6th place to 13th as we jockeyed for position and tested each other out. I was doing my best to keep myself reeled in some and the quick ascent was also doing its part as well (thank you, Quick Ascent.) These first few miles showed me the difference running at a higher elevation could make, as I ran six minutes slower than I had in almost any race to date. I kept telling myself that two-thirds of the race was supposed to be either downhill or flat and that my conservative approach would pay off in the end.

What took us four miles to go up, only took two miles to go back down as it felt like the bottom fell out from underneath us. This controlled fall left most of us winded and again many of us traded places. (There was very little conversation during this race for me. Everyone around me was basically fighting for air). By now, the bright sunshine was beginning to cook us a bit and there was very little shade to be had. Then I missed a mile marker somewhere and mistakenly thought mile 12 was mile 13. Ugh.

Suddenly, I saw a mule deer standing about two feet off of the course watching the runners. He showed no fear whatsoever and stood so still I thought he was a statue until I got closer. Because of the angry elk warning, my personal trepidation was high. Deer goring would significantly hinder my chance of success for the rest of the year. I scampered by as fast as I could.

As was advertised, the highest point of the race was at mile 6. Unfortunately, its two ugly stepsisters were at mile 17-18 and later at mile 22. My only conversation of the race was around mile 16 when a few of us joked about some of the things spectators say as encouragement to runners which then led to a discussion about Fiddy2. A few people dropped off as we climbed a hill with the sun beating down and the wind blowing. I knew at this point the leaders were far ahead and I was really beginning to fade. I was determined to not run in the 3:40s. Already way off my predicted goal times, I just wanted to finish respectably and not pass out. A neat end to the race was 300 meters on the high school track to the applause of a smattering of locals and volunteers.

I will admit that the final six miles was absolutely breathtaking (not a good thing when you are gasping for air.) It became clear to me why, along with talent and training, Kenyans are such superb runners. At home they run at an elevation that deprives them of breathing oxygen-rich air so running at much lower levels makes them winners of the oxygen lottery.

It took me five full minutes of leaning against a wall at the end to simply catch my breath. I then thanked the race director, and hopped in my friend's car for the ride back to Boulder.

In true, Dane-really-hates-airline-travel fashion, my already late flight got delayed again and the person ahead of me wanted to recline onto my lap. I finally got home somewhere around 3 am. The alarm went off at seven the next morning for work. It seemed like one of the worst sounds I had ever heard.

24

Starting to Hurt

Marathon 25
Race: Pacific Crest Marathon, Sunriver, OR
Miles from home: 2780.3
648 miles raced
707.4 miles to go

Finishing Time: 3:16:58
Place: 10th

In a weekend where the marathon could have easily been swallowed up by the other events going on, (the Pacific Crest Endurance Weekend included a Kid's Splash Pedal-n-Dash for kids ages 12 & under, a Half Iron Triathlon, Endurance Duathlon, Marathon, Half-Marathon, an Olympic Distance Triathlon, Olympic Distance Duathlon, 5K & 10K Run/Walks, Kid's Dash), this marathon was anything but an afterthought. The marathon was a smallish one and could have easily taken a back seat to the other events. However, with a water stop seemingly at every mile, this marathon totally passed the Dane Rauschenberg Standard of Adequate Liquid Provision (DR SALP.) But from water to Gatorade to a Red Bull station (this was just fantastic, by the way) if you were thirsty, it was your own fault. Friendly wonderful volunteers made this race an absolute joy even if the spectators were few and far between.

Kudos to Cathy and Cain and many others.

I met my new friend Bob at the airport in Redmond, Oregon and we drove down to Sunriver together. The place was an absolute madhouse. The entire time we were there events were either going on, about to start, or just finished. We quickly got our packets and decided we just had time to grab dinner and go to bed. I had been traveling all day from DC to San Francisco to Oregon and wanted to get a good night's rest. Bob had been driving all day from Southern California and was equally tired.

The Sunriver Marathon people had been nice enough to provide me with lodging and because of Bob's generosity in picking me up at the airport I let him stay in the extra bed I had at my place. I then showered and hit the sack getting more rest than I'd had in quite some time. Too bad conventional wisdom says two nights before the race is the important sleep night. But given the short week of rest (this was a Saturday race) and with this race on the heels of last week's tough Estes Park marathon, I would take the sleep wherever I could get it.

I had noticed in the past few races, it seemed to take me over six miles to actually feel like I might do well in a race. Sunriver was no different. I was beginning to worry that all the travel and elevation running had taken its toll. However, around mile 8 or 9 it seemed my lungs got adjusted and I started feeling fine.

I ran the first half basically alone. A pack of three or four runners shot out of the chute at the gun and about a mile later another cluster passed me. From mile 2 until just about the half-way point, I was running solo on a twisting bike-path type course, (making it difficult to gauge pace) which was virtually spectator-free. As I ran along this path, which criss-crossed through cottages, people walking their dog or having a cup of coffee on their porch would stare at me quizzically. Every once in a great while, when the course looped around a body of water, I would see that second group of runners off in the distance ahead of me. However, other than these brief glimpses, I could have been just another runner out for a solo jog.

Right before the half, I finally caught a guy who I had been tracking down for miles. I had steadily made up ground on this guy and was hoping it was me that was going faster, and not him that was slowing down. But every single mile for four straight miles my pace was exact: 7:20. I mean, on the freaking nose. I actually chuckled when my fourth mile showed that exact same time. Finally passing the guy with a "howdy" and a comment about how the swarm of gnats hitting us in the face were bonus protein, I circled into the staging area. Tons of people were milling around half-cheering, half-getting ready for their own race. I passed the halfway marker to a smattering of applause and the announcer saying: "Here is Dane Rauschenberg on his first lap of the marathon. Dane will be running FIFTY marathons this year!" If not for the fact that I had to dodge some pedestrian who had meandered into the bright-orange, roped-off section that directed runners where to go, I might have stopped and corrected him.

Having passed a straggler from one of the packs in front of me, I was hoping to catch them all and move from what I thought was 12th place to about 6th. However, now seeing a person in the path ahead could mean I was either catching a marathoner in front of me or passing a half-marathoner (they started 30 minutes behind us). I think my stance on slower runners is similar to many other runners but I feel I need to make it clear here. It is an absolute pleasure for me to see Americans out on race day, walking, running, or strolling. With the average citizen pushing the boundaries of obesity, the fact that someone is out there doing anything makes me extremely happy. However, slower runners must respect other runners and do their best to not walk nineteen abreast. I am, of course, using hyperbole but on this particular day, the course was so narrow that when you approached a runner/walker who was in his or her own world, you had no choice but to go off course and run around them. I did my best to make loud stomping noises to alert those I was passing but it was to no avail. Alas.

Now, passing people provides a mental boost, even if you know they are not in your race. And I needed that boost because I went from ticking off exact 7:20 miles to exact 7:36 miles. It was uncanny. No matter how much I felt like I pressed, for five straight miles I had the exact same mile pace. Somewhere in there, one of the cofounders of Marathon Maniacs passed me, and chatted me up a bit. Chris Warren was himself running his twelfth marathon of the year. He asked when I was going to be joining his club. I told him in three more weeks I would be at the second highest level you can obtain in a year (with 24 weeks to go) and at that time I would be joining. I bid him adieu and sunk into a couple of slow miles.

Yet, in spite of this slower pace I was able to pass another runner who I had been slowly gaining on. Soon thereafter, close to mile 25, another guy suddenly appeared ahead of me. I did some quick math in my head and from my calculations, passing him would put me in 10th overall. Plus, he looked like he was my age group and I would be damned if I was going to let a repeat of last week happen. So, I picked up the pace, passed him and streaked into the finish. My math had been right and sure enough I finished 10th overall and second in my age group.

The most memorable meeting of all though, was with a wonderful single mother of three (she said she was 35 but looked about 22) who was running the marathon one year to the day after having heart surgery. This recap goes out to her.

25

Top of the World

Marathon 26
Race: Leadville Trail Marathon, Leadville, CO
Miles from home: 1798.4
681.2 miles raced
681.2 miles to go

Finishing Time: 5:17:41
Place: 49th

Well, that's done.

It would be the biggest understatement of the year to say I experienced extreme travel difficulties prior to competing in the hardest race I have ever attempted. To reiterate would be beating a dead horse, but I never liked Mr. Ed anyway and he must pay. Basically, the entirety of Fiddy2 was put at a great risk when bad business practices left me less than 24 hours to the start of the Leadville marathon sitting nearly 2000 miles away.

I eventually (through effort and a restraint I did not think I possessed) booked a last-minute one-way flight at enormous expense, made the two-hour drive to Leadville with my friends Alyssa and Josh (seeing them for the second time in ten days, which is more than I was seeing some friends who live five minutes away), passed out at the bed & breakfast, got up early to get my race packet pre-race (getting in at 11pm didn't allow me to get it the day before) and stood staring at the Rocky Mountains in awe, wondering what in the Sam Hill I had gotten into. (I had planned to capture this beauty with a digital camera at the halfway point. But unfortunately my fingers must not have worked properly at this elevation. So I carried a camera with me the whole way for one little shot that I found out after the race, never came to fruition. You can imagine my disappointment). Prior to the race, I'd had a wonderful interview with the Denver Post and was extremely flattered they had traveled all the way to the start to speak to me. Then I was surprised by my good friend Bryon, who had made the eight-hour drive from Park City to humble me in this race, just one week after he raced in the famed Western States 100 miler. Needless to say, Bryon is a big, fat, punk.

There is no way around it. The race was tough. In fact, I ran the slowest marathon of my life to this point by over an hour and five minutes. My time here made my first marathon ever of 4:12 look like a land speed record. But of the forty-eight people who beat me in this race, only six were not from Colorado. And I know none of them were in their 26th marathon of their year.

There is nothing like being 50 minutes into a race, covered in sweat, exhausted, and thirsty and then realizing you have only traversed 3.8 miles (this is where the first aid station was located; there are no mile markers). While I knew I had to be beyond conservative and run slow in this race, I didn't realize that there were many times when I would have absolutely no choice. My pre-race plan was to walk/jog the uphills and sprint the downhills and hope the net loss of elevation on the back 13 miles would make up for what was going to be a brutal first half.

At the next aid station (7.1 miles) I found myself next to a wonderful woman from New Jersey who was on her multiple running of Leadville.

"I'm running two Leadville marathons today: my first and my last," I told her.

She laughed, "Wait and see."

"Oh, I'm willing to take bets," I said.

The steady downhill to the next aid station was wonderful until I realized it was going to be an uphill on the way back from miles 16-19. In addition, a horrible leg cramp I had acquired in Estes Park two weeks prior started up around mile 8. I began to wonder what the next 17 miles were going to be. Filling up with liquids at the aid station, I looked up at the three mile, 3,000-foot climb to the halfway point at Mosquito Pass (13,285 feet). I then simply put my head down and began walking/running as fast as I could.

Those next 3 miles would take me an hour to conquer. Doubled over and pushing down on my legs with my arms, there were times when even walking was too much. I would stand straight up, take a five-count breath and continue on. I had been unsure of the weather so I had donned gloves prior to the race as well as removable sleeves. When the sun came out I discarded the sleeves and kept the gloves. I then noticed that by repeatedly using my hands to push down on my legs, I had been rubbing my thighs raw. However, it was not until after the race that I noticed a strip seven inches long on each thigh where no hair remained. Smooth as a baby's bottom. This has to be the oddest "injury" I have ever sustained.

When Bryon came down from Mosquito Pass, he let me know I had about five minutes to the top. As ticked off as I was that he was this far ahead of me, knowing I was close to the top was music to my ears. I crested the halfway point, tried to take the video, ate some watermelon, pretzels, and drank Gatorade and Diet Coke. (The volunteers here were wonderful.) I then turned around for the three-mile sprint/fall, almost an hour and a half slower than I usually run the first half of a marathon.

Sharing the path down with people who were on their way up was made more difficult as the trail was akin to a dry river bed littered with tons of large stones. It was all I could do to let out a "Waytogo!" (all said in one word) in response too those saying "Good job!" as I flew by, arms akimbo, eyes on the path in front of me looking for that one free footfall.

Runners are good people. I am not sure if running attracts good people or if people become good by virtue of running. Regardless, as I am barreling down the hill, rapidly catching people on the narrow pass, it was evident I would overtake some of the runners in front of me. Rather than make me run around them and possibly break my neck, every single runner, more or less stopped, stepped to the side and allowed me to pass by unhindered. I thanked them and assured them I would see them on the uphills.

As I guessed, the run to mile 19 was just a long struggle of power walking as my calf began screaming. I would stop to rub it, run with a straight leg on the left to minimize the muscle usage, and do everything I could to alleviate the pain. But the pain would not go. So I just pressed on.

I stood at the last aid station refilling for the final sprint and could see the city of Leadville in the distance. Thunderstorms had threatened intermittently (and would later drench the area), and there was some wind throughout the day. However, for the most part, the prevailing weather consisted of a blazing sun, which beat down especially hard right here. With one final gasp of air, I took off.

The last few miles were a blur. I knew it would take a Herculean effort to make it in under 5 hours. Carefully picking my steps through the steepest part of the course and eyeing up potential victims who weren't aware I was coming, I am sure I smiled a few times. I knew the pain would soon be over. Within minutes, I found my first victim. I chewed him up and spit him out in half a mile. Two more people stared at me as I leapt around them like a mountain goat. Another person down (although she might have been a half marathoner) left one last person in my sights.

A man with whom I'd had a brief conversation had laid me to waste for six miles. Unfortunately for him there was one mile left. With the first steady wind of the race blowing in our faces, I don't even think he heard my footsteps as I approached. I swear he jumped a bit when his peripheral vision caught me about half a mile to the finish. A fast spoken "Hey, what charity are you running for again?" solicited an even faster "I'll give you a card at the end" as I decided it was time. I kicked it into the highest gear I had left and refused to finish in 5:18.

Alyssa and Josh waited for me at the end and let the announcer know what I was doing. I burst through the finish line. Immediately Bryon, Alyssa and Josh descended on me ready to help. However, even though this race was extremely difficult, I was in better condition than at the end of Estes Park two weeks earlier.

I was now halfway done my task. Unforeseen events had made the task look impossible. I knew more would come. But I knew there was one thing that I could foresee, and that was every weekend, one way or another I would be wearing a finisher's medal.

Topping out at 13,000 plus feet, the Leadville Marathon was both the literal and figurative half-way point of Dane's 52 marathons.

26

Recovery

Marathon 27
Race: Seafair Marathon, Bellevue, WA
Miles from home: 2770.8
707.4 miles raced
655 miles to go

Finishing Time: 3:23:52
Place: 46th

Let me first say this. Leadville took more out of me than I cared to admit, even to myself.

I packed a lot into my brief stay in the greater Seattle area. First, I met a good friend for the first time in real life (a person can undoubtedly be a good friend even if you have never met them in person, believe me), met other running friends and also got to see another friend, Devon, in a documentary about her high school basketball team in Seattle. Throw in a little sightseeing and before I knew it, time had come to hit the sack and get ready for the downside of the Fiddy2 Mart honing hill.

I decided before the race to go slow. My left calf was still quite tender after the dual Colorado marathons and I was hoping if I went out a little slower than usual I would have energy at the end to take advantage of the supposed five—mile downhill leading to the finishing line.

Almost exactly to my liking, I sauntered up to the start line about two minutes before the race. No milling around, no people to bump into, no jostling, no wasted energy. My good friend Todd, with whom I was staying, was running the first leg of the relay marathon (just one week before a 200—mile bike ride from Seattle to Portland) so we kissed goodbye (no, not really) and headed to the start. The gun went off and I tried desperately to keep myself in check. It was already a slightly warm and muggy day and the sun was shining bright ahead (not a typical Seattle day, that is for sure). Chris Warren, the co-founder of Marathon Maniac passed me within the first few miles. I held my ground, let him pass me and did my best to continue on at a nice slow pace. Too slow. I tried to pick up the pace but I simply could not make up time. Miles ticked away and my splits stayed the same.

Right before the halfway point I met and ran with Gayle Zorrilla. I had met her briefly in Pacific Crest two weeks ago (where she was the third overall woman). As a Marathon Maniac, she was on her sixth marathon in just six weeks time and one heck of a runner. As we hit a series of hills, I had a little more energy than she did so I told her I was sure I would see her later in the race and away I went.

After the half I felt good. We were running a net downhill and I was taking it nice and easy. However, my calf and quad on my left side were touch and go at best. I figured the downhills would shake both of them loose like in previous races. But then suddenly, I began to just seep energy out of every pore. Then I ran into some uphills that did me in.

Soon thereafter, I hit a long downhill. I closed my eyes to a mere slit and I actually think I fell asleep. I seemed to be in a trance. Next thing I know I was at the bottom.

Chris Warren appeared in my sights and I saw that I was steadily catching him. And here is where the mystery begins. He was wearing a bright yellow singlet so it was really easy to track him, which I had been doing for miles. Then he disappeared. I was not sure if I fell asleep again, if he'd pulled really far ahead or if he'd dropped out.

True to my prediction, with about a mile or so to go, Gayle came along beside me looking surprisingly strong. I told her I was fading, still feeling the effects of Leadville. She gave me a look, which can be summed up in two words: "No duh." She streaked ahead and finished sixth overall for the women (Go Gayle!)

A few more people passed me on another uphill to the finish. I honestly did not care. I was spent. With the final yards on a downward slope, I streaked through the chutes and notched another marathon done. Only upon looking at the results at the end did I notice that Chris did indeed finish, just a few minutes behind me. When and how I passed him is beyond me.

No words of wisdom or great thoughts came to my head. I was ready to sleep.

27

29.2 Miles

Marathon 28
Race: Paul Bunyan Marathon, Bangor, ME
Miles from home: 680
733.6 miles raced
628.8 miles to go

Finishing Time: 3:26:14
Place: 21st

Now more than halfway done, all I was hoping for was to be able to run the marathons each weekend. I was not asking for much.

However, for the second time in as many weeks, the shuttle service was late picking me up. I took matters into my own hands. I hopped in my car and sped (seriously) to the airport. Getting there, I realized I had never parked at the airport before. Ever. I had no idea where to go. So, now I had to find the lot.

I did, but then had to wait for a shuttle to take me to the terminal. Once in the terminal I hurried to my line and stood there, shaking. The line was long, and time was short. I thought I might as well try the machines. However, they were full as well, so I went back to my line. The ticket person, wielding that small amount of power she had over me (is there anything worse than people like this?) told me I had to wait in line. The line I had just been in. When I tried to tell her I had in fact been in line, she waved her hand at me. I finally lost my cool and told her (loudly) I did not need her waving her hand at me. She grabbed her little bedazzled purse, turned some key on her desktop and walked away, closing the door behind her. Now, not only was she screwing me over but the entire line behind me as well. Only after a few passengers intervened to tell the American Airlines personnel (who now had appeared behind me) that I had, in fact, done everything asked of me, did I get service. However, by now, I had missed my flight. They booked me onto a later flight to LaGuardia, which would then connect to Bangor. This snafu caused me to miss a scheduled interview to promote Fiddy2 and a chance to convince people to donate.

So I sat in the terminal and fumed. And fumed. I know few people who can really cultivate a good "fume" like me. I laugh (maniacally, mind you) at the people who tell me they could run a marathon every week. "Hey, you know what?" I think. "They probably could." But no one (including myself) could have anticipated all the extemporaneous things, which would pop up every weekend, all potentially preventing me from achieving my goal.

I do not envy those who are the race directors for a marathon. It is an arduous task, with roadblocks at every turn and events beyond your control that threaten constantly to end in disaster. However, there are many things they have to do correctly or complaints are going to fly.

Which gets me to the marathon. There was nothing exceedingly wrong with this marathon. Unfortunately, there was nothing exceedingly right either. This opinion is obviously not about the persons who ran the marathon, of course. Almost every race director I have met is a wonderful person. However, wonderful people can sometimes make bad decisions.

Before I get to that, I was just happy to finally be in my hotel. As I was checking in, I ran into Bob and Lenore Dolphin, wonderful supporters of many marathons, runners of even more and the organizers of the Yakima River Marathon. We chatted for what had to have been over an hour without me even unpacking my bag. After I helped Bob figured out his shower (yet another contraption from hell), I ran into one friend and met two new ones. Cowboy Jeff Bishton (who was sharing a room with me) showed up and we chatted a bit before we went to the pasta dinner. I must have met about 10-15 people I had either seen before or who had heard of me because of Fiddy2. I was feeling great. Luckily the warmth of the company filled our bellies as the one shot and you are done, no refills $15 pasta dinner left a hole in the belly.

I was lucky enough to reschedule my interview for the local news and met with the reporter for a bit. After that it was time to head back to the hotel and catch forty winks. It had been a long day.

After a few more interviews with the wonderful local media (including a fol-low-up interview with one great guy who, the previous day had showed me where Stephen King lives) the race was ready to begin. It was already getting very warm and muggy and I felt we were in for a rough day. One thing that bothered me was the fact that no one who did not live in the area knew what to expect on the course. I broke a personal oath to never run a race that has no elevation chart on the website. It is a recipe for disaster.

The pain I had in my calf muscle from the Colorado marathons was ever pres-ent these days. While I continue to get it worked on, it still nagged. What little pre-race knowledge of the course I had was that, it being Maine, hills would abound. Therefore, my race-time decision was to, once again, nurse the legs, run conservatively, and see what I had at the end.

A few miles in, after seeing my old friend Rob Toonkel for the first time in almost two months and a man dressed as a pink fairy (more on that later), nature called. The complete lack of porta-potties proved to be a pain. So I took what some called "the long-cut through the woods". Soon, I was out of the woods and back running with Rob but I could tell that the heat was al-ready getting to me. I, unfortunately, was no fan of the energy drink provided, so staying hydrated was quite a challenge. An early morning fog had either turned into rain or was so low-hanging that there was no difference. Staying cool became a difficult task in the humidity and the CONSTANT rolling hills were not helping.

As in most the cases this year, my second 13.1 miles is usually less excit-ing than anything previously. The crowd thins out, the runners become more sparse and usually I begin to think about self-preservation mode where...IS THAT ANOTHER HILL? (Sorry. Flashback.) Well, this time I had a nagging pride issue to deal with when the very athletic (yet very pink) fairy passed me at mile 16 or so (along with my friend Greg who I had first met at Hatfield & McCoy a few weeks ago). I had hoped that the pink fairy would not be a problem today but it was not to be. Exacting revenge for my beating him in Delaware, PF put me to shame in the final 10 miles. Yukking it up at the end we traded some barbs. He mentioned how he had crushed me today and I pointed out he had done one third the marathons I had.

As I have said before, I am unsure which came first in the chicken and the egg scenario of marathoning, but runners, by and large are good, kind and generous people. I think I made ten new friends here in the Pine Tree State and I know I told many more about Fiddy2.

But there was still more to go. You see I had to walk nearly three miles from the finish line back to the start where our car was parked. Shuttle service to the staring line, which was supposed to be there, never appeared. And I had a plane to catch. So, a weekend that started with bad transportation, ended with bad transportation.

But I got to discover a family owned restaurant named Pizza Oven on my trot back. Given my hunger and the timing, this pizza was just about the best food I had tasted in a long time. And since I had two teeth removed the prior week to help the braces settle in, its softness and gooey cheese were music to my ...teeth? So if you are in Bangor I totally recommend Gary, Katie and Gary Jr.'s place.

28

Braving Beryl

Marathon 29
Race: Nova Scotia Marathon, Barrington, NS
Miles from home: 811
759.8 miles raced
602.6 miles to go

Finishing Time: 3:19:25
Place: 3rd

Thursday before the marathon, I had the chance to run in a non-marathon race for the first time since the Goofy Challenge in January. For only 5 bucks, 7 miles from my house, I took a stab at a local 8k. My legs felt better than they had in weeks, so I wanted to give them a final test with some semi-sprinting. In addition, since weekly routine had been work, travel, run, (lather, rinse, repeat) for months, I was aching for some variety. I ran a very evenly paced race and felt great.

Fast forward to Friday afternoon where Kathy (my travel companion for the weekend) and I were one of the last flights to land amidst fog, rain and storms that day in Canada (thank you, Tropical Storm Beryl!)

A remote interview with CBC television awaited me in the drizzle of the airport's parking lot. After this, we hopped into my rental car to begin the harrowing three-hour drive from Halifax to Barrington (thank you, Tropical Storm Beryl!) By the time we checked into our B&B, we were quite exhausted. Flipping on the TV for some background noise while we unpacked, we had just enough time to realize that the news reporter was going into my taped interview on CBC. I can't tell you how neat it was to see this. And once again, I received great press for Fiddy2 north of the border. Canada dug my running.

Soon, we had met some of the others in the B&B who were also running one of the races (half or full), including Simon, a delightful English chap who was hoping for his first marathon finish. Not long after that, our beds called our names and we were sleeping.

The next day broke with more of the same dreary, chilly, windy weather. Assured by the locals that this was NOT typical weather (I think they were all on the local tourism board, which was really not necessary given how gorgeous Nova Scotia is) we decided to make the best of the day. We went to the Barrington Curling club (what an odd sport) to get my race packet. At the table where I got my number I learned that if you had brought your own drinks for use on the course, you could label them with your bib number and they would place them in boxes to be distributed at all of the spots where fluids were handed out. Talk about personal attention!

I drove the marathon course for one of the first times ever prior to a race. Kathy and I took in some sights and checked out a reproduction lighthouse, had some decent pasta at the pasta dinner, chatted with some other racers and prepped for the next day. Howling winds (gusts up to 50 mph, at least) kept me up that night.

While the rain had slowed, the wind did not. The race started a little later than most of mine this year (8:30 am), which held threats of possible warm temperatures in spite of the otherwise inclement weather. Following half-marathoners for the first 9.5 miles, I could see there were only a few racers in front of me. When the two races split, my suspicions were confirmed. While my legs were still a little weary from the year of, well, everything and my left calf was far from perfect, I knew I could hang with a few of these guys for a while. That is, if the wind did not kill me.

122

In one of the most constant, steady and energy-sapping winds I have run in, I kept wondering how much easier this run would have been if I just had someone to draft off of. Then around mile 11, I noticed a very fit woman behind me who had slowly been gaining ground. I had been warned pre-race that two elite Canadian ultra marathoners were running this race, one male and one female. I had met the male runner (and he had been in front of me since about foot 2 of the race) and by the looks of it, I was about to meet the female.

We turned onto an out-and-back portion of the race named "the Hawk"; we had been warned that although this is the second southern-most point in Canada it is quite blustery and could be 10 15 degrees colder here than anywhere else in the race. While not colder, we were definitely running, once again, into steady headwind. Not until we approached the turn around, which was literally feet away from the shoreline, did the wind finally blow at our backs. In addition, having noticed that the woman behind me had fallen off the pace a bit, I was in pretty good spirits. I was beginning to think of how exciting it might be to actually place in the top three in this race. But with so much more racing to go, I crammed that thought away. All around us was ocean and land that might be gorgeous on a normal day but the dense fog kept us from actually enjoying the beautiful scenery.

Throughout the race, Kathy had met me every few miles with both supplies and updates on other runners. While rainy and windy, the course was deceptively hot and I needed all the fluids she was able to give me. Twice I had actually taken off my shirt to ring it out. Kathy kept me abreast of the female behind me.

Mile 20 was rapidly approaching and I remembered from my drive the day before that a big hill loomed here. I took a quick glance behind me, and lo and behold, the very fit woman had caught me! I had never even heard her as she approached (swirling winds made any noise behind you almost impossible to hear) but she must have been slowly closing the gap since The Hawk four miles back. Damn it.

I took off. I could not help it. I thought if I was going to get beaten, I was going to make the racer work for it. Yet, in spite of how much I sped up, the very fit woman stayed right behind me.

Finally, at mile 23, I couldn't hold her off anymore. All sinew and tanned muscle, very fit woman passed me on an uphill. I stayed within striking distance for the next mile but at the hill on 25 (damn you hill!) I just didn't have it in me anymore. I looked behind me and saw a guy we had both passed had disappeared. I was all alone in the fog.

Taking it easy down the last hill and across the causeway off the island to the mainland where the finish was, I knew I could make a run for both the people in front of me. But once again I kept the big picture in mind and realized that if I hurt myself in that final sprint, I would fall short of my goal for Fiddy2. So I reeled it in and amidst the cheers of some hearty folk braving the rain I cruised in to the finish. Hardly a blistering time, my 3:19:25 was however, my first sub 3:20 in three weeks and given the conditions, one I was rather pleased with.

In addition, since the elite man and that elite woman were the only two people who finished in front of me, I had my first ever "place": 3rd overall. I could not have been more happy. So after some congratulatory handshakes, it was back to the B&B for a quick shower, then off again on a 3-hour drive to the airport where, of course, both flights were delayed. I love getting home at 1 am.

A sign on the way to the Nova Scotia Marathon provided for the perfect
photo opportunity.

29

Rock Then Glaciers

Marathon 30
Race: San Francisco Marathon, San Francisco, CA
Miles from home: 2810.5
786 miles raced
576.4 miles to go

Finishing Time: 3:19:44
Place: 148th

As one may guess, it has been either feast or famine with me this year with regards to when I get to see other runner friends. At this race it was feast. From a group of runners getting together for a pre-race carb loading dinner (many who were "meeting" for the first time, even though they would probably all consider each other friends), to my hosts for this weekend, Jenni and Devon (who had to split up time with me, because, well, I am a handful) to those I did not get to see until I was actually running the race, it was a jam—packed weekend.

From the very inception of Fiddy2, the San Francisco Marathon and its organizers were extremely receptive and helpful in getting the word out about my being the only person running a real marathon every single weekend this year. Mentioned along with Dean Karnazes on their website as a "featured runner" (a true honor), this white-glove treatment continued even further. Upon receiving my packet at the expo, I realized I was privileged enough to receive an "elite" bib number, one that would be easy to remember: 52. While this "elite" status (which made me sort of feel like a fraud; I know my place in the marathoning pecking order) would put me in the first wave of runners to start the race, I knew I wouldn't stay there for long. Normally, I might have been able to justify this status to some degree with a pace that would have earned the bib, but not in my 30th marathon of the year.

After a very long flight to San Francisco on Friday, too little sleep that night, an interview with a wonderful woman at Reuters after the expo (where I got to see Dean K) and the pasta dinner in our bellies, Jenni and I were ready for an early bedtime. Tired as we were and knowing we had to wake up at 4 am didn't make going to bed when it was still very much light out, any easier. But sleep we did and our alarms woke us seemingly only minutes after we laid our heads down to sleep.

We grabbed a cab to the start (we were not going to rely on intermittent buses this early in the morning); I got to see how alive San Francisco was at this early hour. I battled "women of the night" for our ride. I hugged Jenni goodbye and wished her good luck, before mingling with the others in Corral Number One. Nervous energy permeated the atmosphere in the corral. Here and there a lone woman broke up the crowd of male faces, and all wore looks of determination. I realized how calm I was and how used to the pre-race drama I had become. Some people do their grocery shopping on Sunday; I race a marathon.

We would be starting in waves five minutes apart, to keep gridlock off the Golden Gate Bridge. I knew Jenni would be starting much later than I and I probably wouldn't see much of her. In addition, I knew that those in the wave right behind me would probably be catching me a few miles after the start, as I would be running my more conservative pace once again.

The time drew near, the pack grew tight together on the timing mat and with a rather surprising "Go!" shouted by someone as the start (rather than a gun, doves, fireworks, horn, siren, cannon or something else), we were off. I realized I had not been in a marathon of this size since Miami in January. In fact, my previous eight marathons combined did not have the number of finishers that would cross the line in the next seven hours. In spite of my desire to go slow I still found myself running faster than I should. So much fast, in fact, that the 3 hour pace group (6:52 minute mile) took over three miles to catch me. Damn you, adrenaline and competitive nature!

I did my best to let those pass me and run my own race (a phrase I tell many when asked for advice). I knew the majority of the hills of this race were supposed to be in the first half, so I set my mind to running decently fast but conservatively at first and hope to really push it home on the downhills to the finish.

Around mile 7, and after a big hill, we began crossing the Golden Gate Bridge. Through a slight fog, the large red spans loomed in front of us. Off to the right, Alcatraz sat forebodingly.

The fog around us was a welcome sun-blotter as the Bay Area had just a few days earlier experienced record-breaking heat. In fact, when Jenni and I caught the cab to the race in the morning we both commented on how nice it was to feel a slight chill. However, as I crossed the bridge, I realized I was sweating profusely. It neither felt hot nor was the sun beating down on me. Hoping this was just the fog, I still made a mental note to be careful with my fluids. I refused to bonk this day.

After crossing the bridge, I made a small loop through a parking lot before I prepared to cross its majestic span once again. Policing this turn and manning the water station were some heavily leather-clad bikers. Not only were they at this turn near the bridge but at multiple intersections of the course. In past races, I have seen people try to skirt past police officers directing traffic and almost get hit by some oblivious motorist. But no one was ignoring directions from my new favorite traffic stoppers. Yet, in spite of their appearance, they were all so darn friendly! As I crossed I found I was virtually running alone on my half of the road. The pack I had started with was clumped together in front of me and slowly pulling away. The pack behind me had not yet made up their five-minute deficit. As hordes of people streamed by on the other side of the bridge, I felt like I was running in the wrong direction. However, running alone had its advantages. Namely, all my friends who I had not seen at the start could easily identify me. Cowboy Jeff, Greg and Z all picked me out and cheered me on. So did Devon, who, while pacing her sister in her first marathon ever (finishing in a time well under four hours: Go Super Squirroll), did some sort of cheerleader jumpkick in excitement as she cheered me on. I am surprised she did not pull something.

A few more hills and turns and I had reached the halfway point. Slightly slower than I expected, I had hopes for a faster second half.

The second half of the race held fewer interesting stories. This gave me a lot of time to realize runners behind me didn't need to pass me to "beat" me time-wise, because of the wave starts. So I pressed on a little harder than I normally would. While I was still covered in sweat and the fog had burned off as the sun began to peek through the clouds, I still felt relatively good. Some leg pain, some tiredness but nothing that foretold of any major crash at the end. And to kill the suspense, that crash never came. But then again, neither did the consistent downhills reported to bring up the rear of the race.

I passed mile 25 and then the ballpark where the Giants play (Lord knows what conglomerate owns its naming rights now.) The last flat homestretch was in sight. Sprinting by a few people (who were probably in the wave behind me anyway) I pushed it home as the announcer called out my name: "Dane Rauschenberger." Rauschenberg is long enough as it is; I really don't think I need two more letters.

The race was over, I had another sub 3:20. I sunk my tender teeth into a cheese and tortilla enchilada given out at the end, one of the best post-race foods I have ever had. I thank my friend Mike for grabbing two of these for me.

But as tired as I was (and I was tired) I had promised Jenni I would do my best to go back, find her and run the rest of her race with her. So, I threw my finisher's medal over my neck and headed back towards the course. Ever a multi-tasker, I used this time to call my parents and let them know how I had fared.

I found Jenni just after mile 25. She looked great! On a course that was far from easy she was on pace to set a personal best! So I jumped in with her, handed her some fluid and did my best to be as least annoying as possible. Soon after I joined Jenni we were caught by another friend who, having suffered some cramps, was finishing slightly slower than he wished. But now the three of us were running abreast, all the way home. Pulling out of the chutes with about 100 yards to go, I began running alongside Jenni through the crowd the best I could, with one hand on my stopwatch and the other on my finisher's medal as it bounced off my chest. Leaving nothing to chance, she crossed the line almost 2 minutes faster than her previous best!

On a challenging course that had made for a difficult race for a few friends, we were all pleased to be finished and enjoy a gorgeous San Francisco day. After a flight from San Francisco to Indianapolis, to Atlanta to my "final destination" of D.C., (that's what you have to do when you buy cheap tickets!) I laid my head on my pillow around 1:30 am and fell deeply asleep.

My first trip ever to our 49th state loomed. Unfortunately, with the marathon on Saturday, I followed up the long flight from San Francisco to DC with the longer flight to Alaska on a short week's rest. Who scheduled this thing?

Marathon 31
Race: Frank Maier Marathon, Juneau, AK
Miles from home: 2599
812.2 miles raced
550.2 miles to go

Finishing Time: 3:16:50
Place: 5th

Someone will have to explain to me someday the logistics of how a plane can be oversold. I mean, I know why. (The airlines never want an empty seat on a flight as it costs them money.) But how? Is there any other business in the world where this idea is feasible, let alone legal? I cannot sell my car to Steve on Thursday and hope that he does not pick it up when he wants to because I sold it to Sally the next day. And when Steve does show up, I cannot tell him that I will get him a car the next day, but not the car I sold him. "What, Steve? You needed to have that car this very afternoon because this was the day you go in to have your brain, liver, kidney, spinal column transplant, which is why you bought it three months ago? I am sorry about that but there is nothing I can do. You did not 'check-in' to pick up the object you already paid for. So, here is a voucher for some overpriced crappy food at my house. Thank you for your patience. I apologize for the delay."

Juneau: I have a feeling it is gorgeous. Lush and green, mountains nestled right up next to rivers. Thin rivulets of waterfalls cascading down the side of the hills like pieces of string on a green felt background. Hilltops and mountains that touch the sky. I mean, I think they touch the sky. There is a sky, right? You see a place does not get this lush and green without its fair share of rainfall. Unfortunately, its fair share came the weekend I was there and it came in buckets. A steady drizzle punctuated by random downpours soaked the Juneau area the entire time. But I will say this: the volunteers and workers of the marathon were completely undeterred and some of the friendliest people I have met. Serious kudos go to people who stood out in rain slickers for hours directing traffic and handing out water and food.

One thing is for sure about Juneau; it is expensive. Do not ask me about the hotel prices or how much a Subway meatball sub meal deal costs because they are more than you would expect. Luckily for me, I had a friend who lives in Juneau (he and his fiancée and daughter were wonderful hosts) so the uber-pricey plane ticket was the most I paid this weekend.

We were warned that the course (a 13.1 mile out-and-back run completely on a highway) contained its fair share of rolling hills. The website even gave excellent descriptions of the total ascent and descent of each major hill. What we were not expecting (or rather hoping against) were the chilly temps, rain and fog. (What is it with fog? I had run in fog for four consecutive weekends even though I had traveled to almost ever corner of North America.) As most of the nation sweltered in a heat wave I was happy for the cooler temps. And at the beginning of the race, the weather was actually quite nice. The chill in the air and our muscles soon evaporated as we took off into the mist at the sound of the gun.

From the beginning, I could see five people vying for the top three spots. The question was who exactly would get what spot? It would be a battle most of the day.

The rain came steadily as we traversed the first few miles. But as the temperature stayed pretty even, I actually felt good. Two gentlemen passed me. One said he was using this as a training run for the Chicago Marathon and would probably take the first eight miles at a 7:15 pace and then taper off.

Runners are wonderful people. But during races they lie. They lie to themselves and they lie to others. They lie as if their lives depended on it. I am no different. But if a runner tells you he is going to run slow, he is not going to run slow. This guy was no different and as I averaged 7:15s for much more than eight miles, he steadily disappeared into the foggy distance.

Cresting a large but not unmanageable hill I found that another runner had tracked me down. Some young whippersnapper had been reeling me in and as we grabbed drinks from the aid station at the turn around point, he passed me by. I knew I was in either fourth or fifth place but which one I could not be sure. I was wondering if I should stay with this young kid and make a run at third place or if I should not worry because even if I did pass him I would still be in fourth. I decided to just run my own race. I had already placed in a marathon this year, which was more than I could ever have hoped coming into Fiddy2.

Coming down the big hill, the view was quite breathtaking and I forgave the race director for calling the race "scenic". I also noticed the rain had stopped, a big plus given that the temperature in this little area was easily five degrees cooler than everywhere else on the course.

I had seen Lying Runner coming down the hill at the turn-around, but now he was nowhere to be seen. I knew the leader was far in front but was almost certain there was another guy in front of us and that he was beginning to fade. So, I decided to stay just a little behind Young Gun and see what developed in the next few miles.

Unfortunately, rain again developed, and developed with a vengeance. But I knew I could handle this. A lull in my energy from miles 15-18 had disappeared and I found myself running with new fervor. I was actually on a pace to set a new Fiddy2 PR. I had closed the gap on Young Gun even though he had not slowed at all.

Then the wind picked up. Always present during the course, it had not been a huge problem until mile 20. As the slogan goes, a marathon is a 10k race with a 20-mile warm-up. However, much to my chagrin, this 10k race was going to be run directly into a stand-you-up-straight headwind. In addition, I was now passing early-starter marathoners, had half-marathoners coming at me, and was being passed by runners in some shorter distance race as well. Needless to say, the shoulder of the road was getting crowded.

Trying to say "good job" to as many people as I could I plodded along, the wind sapping me. Up ahead, I could also see one rather exuberant woman who "flashed" runners as they passed (she had tights on under her running skirt), and cheered and kicked. She was undoubtedly a beacon of light to other runners but for Grumpy Wet Dane she was simply an obstacle with unpredictably flailing arms and legs. Sure enough, as I approached her to pass, she came to a dead stop, swerved to her left, mooned some on-comers and almost got pancaked by me. She received a very blue version of "please make yourself more aware of your surroundings, gentle miss," as I did my best pirouette to keep from falling.

Mile 24 loomed. Only two more to go. I started to kick as best I could, not 100% sure but thinking that the final 2 miles were completely flat. Interesting how a road I had run on just three hours earlier had become a blank canvas in my mind. Unfortunately, my memory failed me and one last small hill waited at mile 25. As I passed the mile marker, a little blue rocket passed me. "What-in-the..." is what I think I actually said out loud. It turns out this was the very first half-marathoner who went sprinting by me as if he was on mile two. With the end nearing, I put it into whatever gear I had left, went around a corner and prepared to be done. Much to my dismay, the start line was not the finish line but rather the 26-mile mark and we still had .2 to go.

Even though I wanted to knock out every time between 3 and 3:30. I had been doing a horrible job at it. I would get too competitive at the end and I would sprint to a time I already had. But one time I did not have was a 3:17. However, again, I could not hold back, and pushed ahead to a 3:16;50, and fifth place overall (I am glad I had not pushed too hard earlier to catch Young Gun). What was odd was that this was the fifth time I had run a 3:16 this year. It was becoming almost biblical.

Dane: 3:16 For God so loved comic relief and pratfalls that he gave the world Dane.

30

Honoring the Finn

Marathon 32

Race: Paavo Nurmi Marathon, Hurley, WI
Miles from home: 1120.6
838.4 miles raced
524 miles to go

Finishing Time: 3:18:11
Place: 27th

Because bullet points are fun:

- No, that's fine, take it. I didn't want to have Body Glide to keep me from chafing. Thanks for making sure the aircraft was safe from my running lubricant, Airline Industry.

- No Fog? Is that allowed for me this year?

- The lighting of the Paavo Torch the night before the race, with the releasing of balloons to honor the memory of a young Hurley girl taken far too early, was a very emotional ceremony.

- If some runners tell you a course is the hardest they have ever run and others shrug at its difficulty you can safely assume the middle ground of their reactions is a fairly accurate representation of its difficulty.

The weekend started when a local running group brought an Olympic style torch to the town square area. They had run relay style from the beginning of the course and capped off their run by lighting a much bigger torch at the town square. I was especially tired from traveling (due to the averted terrorist attack the day before in London, security had been beefed up at airports everywhere) I knew I could not miss this wonderful display. It was extremely touching to see kids who care. But soon I was headed to bed. The race did not have that early a start time, but it was a point-to-point course. I would have to catch a ride with the race director's family (wonderful, hospitable people) to Upson, WI for the start.

Once there and mingling with a few runners, I realized that they were all wearing something I was not: an ankle bracelet chip timer. Whoops! Usually, you get these chips at the packet pickup. But here at "The Paavo" (what the marathon, named after racing legend Paavo Nurmi, is affectionately called in this area) I had to pick it up at the start line. So, with five minutes until the gun, I sauntered over to a timing table and easily found my bracelet, as it was one of the last few left. Notice I did not say "the last", meaning I was not the biggest dunderhead in America's Dairy Land that morning.

I had met a young fella the night before named Sam Ryder who was hoping to run the time I had been consistently hitting this year. As we waited for the start, Sam asked, "Mind if I run with you?"

"The more the merrier, I said. "I'm going to be running my own race but if you can hang with me, I would welcome your company."

With the first few miles of The Paavo containing slightly more downhills than up, it was not until mile 5 that Sam caught up to me. We knocked off mile after mile together including the supposed worst hill of the race. Winding through small towns, Ma and Pa EveryPerson came out on their porches to cheer us on. Sam had written his name on the front of his shirt, so we were getting many "Go Sam!" cheers as we passed by. Every time they cheered for him, Sam would say: "No, cheer for Dane!" I told him I would rather have donations and we both laughed.

Somewhere on our climb up the three-mile hill (which while challenging was far from brutal), we had a nice young lady lamprey onto us. She asked if she could pace with us; we told her we were happy to have the company. You see, when your running companions include a guy with a name on his shirt and a pretty girl, you get lots of cheers. I know how to pick my racing partners.

The pretty girl's name was Nicole. This was her first long run in a very long time. She was doing the first half of the two-person relay (there was also a five-person relay, and to be honest, when those people pass you, you sort of want to trip them) and greatly appreciated us "pacing her". We told her we were happy to oblige. Finally around mile 12, she wished us luck and pushed it into the relay exchange point about 20 seconds ahead of us. Way to work it, Nicole!

For the next three miles Sam and I ran virtually alone. Sam's father and step-mother met him every few miles to give him water, Gatorade or a towel. Sam graciously offered me everything they gave to him and a few times I accepted. Like clockwork, his parents would grab the things we discarded and meet up with us a few miles later. However, since course logistics made it impossible for them to continue to follow and make it back to the finish on time, the Ryders had to leave.

Sam mentioned at mile 18 that this was where he had faltered in previous races. I told him he would be just fine and to listen to his body. If he needed to slow down, then slow down. We both walked through the water station to rehydrate before starting up again. It has always amazed me what a fifteen second walking break can do to help you regain energy.

This water station marked the end of a solid stretch of miles that were flat and straight. At one point we passed over the Flambeau Flowage, a lake that the causeway of land we were running on cut through. Now we were facing a few more hills. I will say this: the Paavo has everything in terms of terrain: from rolling hills to straight-aways to long, slow, hills to steep, short hills. Here Sam fell back and I began my run alone.

I knew this last stretch would be tough. With the bright sun overhead and no one to pace off of, only one thing made the miles go by at all: water stations at each of the last 6 miles. While at the beginning of the race the water stations were every 2.5 miles or so, starting at mile 18, volunteers handed out water, sponges and Gatorade every mile to the finish. That is what I call a brilliant race director.

Having refused to run a 3:17 the week before, I was only hoping to be able to do so here. Unfortunately, Cemetery Hill was making me work for it.

I turned the last corner, saw the bright blue finish line banner and started sprinting. And for the first time since June, this push did not immediately make me fear I would rupture my calf muscle. Unfortunately, today was not meant to be. I was not going to get a 3:17, so I eased up over the last 100 yards to avert injury and crossed in 3:18:11.

Because of flight schedules I was actually able to stick around and enjoy some of Hurley, including the post-race festivities held in a nearby park, shaded by trees with a wonderful cover band playing in the background. I received my award for 1st place in my age group. Virtually matching the excellent finisher's medal, the age group award was just as wonderful.

My friend Jack and I drove to Lake Superior, took tons of photos and ate at this rustic restaurant called the Kimball Inn (I had seafood tortellini; damn, it was good!). At the Dairy Queen for dessert we ran into some of the members of the band who had played at the awards ceremony. Like virtually everyone else I met in Hurley and surrounding area, they were affable people. Way to go, Badger State citizens!

By the way, Sam finished in 3:21 – more than four minutes faster than his previous best. Excellent work, fella. Hope you enjoyed the stew at the end,

31

Running Through Sand and Thin Air

Marathon 33
Race: Silver State Marathon, Washoe City, NV
Miles from home: 2610.9
864.6 miles raced
497.8 miles to go

Finishing Time: 3:22:30
Place: 6th

The airline industry basically got it right this time. On my eighty-first through eighty-fourth flights of the year I wasn't thoroughly disgusted. Kudos. This marathon had some of the prettiest volunteers this year. No idea why but it was nice. But scenic just wasn't doing it for me anymore. Maybe if I was running slower.

It was folly to think that I could produce the same result every week, regardless of what happened that week at work, or the weather I was running in, the course I was running on or where the race took place. I 'follied' in the greater Reno area and felt I should have done better than I did without taking into account mitigating circumstances.

First off, my body was acting very weird. I was not hungry all day Saturday and only had a burger and chips for lunch. I did not eat dinner and barely had anything to drink. Second, I was wiped out. I had been up at 4:30 am to catch my flight on Saturday (and 4:30 am for the race and 4:30 for my return flight; my life rocks!) and when I crashed at 7 pm I had been up for 18 hours. Still, I just wasn't expecting to be so beat. Third, upon waking race day I was neither hungry nor thirsty but forced myself to eat and drink. I could not figure out why any of these things were happening.

A drive in complete darkness to a place that wasn't exactly on the map was made much easier when I began following a line of four or five cars all making the same random turns in the Nevada desert. I figured I was going to either end up at the starting line or at a drug deal. Luckily, it was the former.

I had just enough time at the starting line to meet a gentleman I had been chatting with online about this race. He said he was shooting for a sub 3:35 and I told him anything sub 3:17 would please me. An older chap I had met in numerous races was honored for making his fifth time around all the states (giving him a minimum of 250 marathons run) Pretty amazing. There was just as much applause for him as there was for a man who had dropped 100 lbs in the past year and was celebrating his new health by running his first marathon. With just over 100 runners at the starting line the personal side was a pleasant touch.

Right from the start I could tell we were at elevation. While I had run at almost identical elevation in Sunriver, Oregon a few weeks prior, this course was not mostly flat. From the first mile, when we hit the initial incline, I noticed my lungs were working even harder. In addition, I had noticed something was wrong with the way I had been breathing through. The combination of the two made me feel a little light-headed. It turns out I had, and still have, a large perforation in my septum. Operable but almost not worth it. However, as per the norm this year, after about five miles, I caught my breath and things seemed to settle in nicely. I had high hopes.

While a flat straightaway on the road for a few miles allowed for a little solace, the advertised sand trail through a desert-like area followed. The sand was not free flowing like you would find at the beach but it was definitely not hard-packed either. Trying to run in the few footprints left by those who ran before me, I spent half the time stabilizing myself as the sun started to shine down from above.

After the sand trails the course turned into an orienteering exercise. Running on another sand trail through a barren treeless desert with scrub brush on both sides, I saw no one and heard less. The only person I had caught a glimpse of a few times had long since vanished. Then again, with the twists and turns and high shrubs, he could have been fifty feet in front of me and I would not have known. Every time the course popped out onto a road, I rejoiced to see a white painted arrow telling me I had made the right choices through the labyrinth. But then almost immediately we would veer off of the road and plunge right back into the desert.

A winding, twisting part of the course had me running through a trailer park. There we ran well over 1.5 miles in only a half-mile square area as we looped back and forth. At one trailer there was actually a hand-painted sign which said: "Runners: Be Quiet." Honestly, how much noise do runners make? When we turned back onto the highway out of this area a little past the half-way point, I was relieved.

Coming out of some more loops I saw I had about five minutes on the next person behind me. This emboldened me and I gained a little spring in my step. Before I knew it, I saw a runner appear in front of me. I realized this was a guy who had been in third at one point. As I passed him he mentioned it was his first marathon and he had gone out too fast. I told him it was my forty-fifth, and you never learn. We shared a laugh and away I went.

I was once again running by my lonesome. A few twists and turns and ups and downs, punctuated with the occasional truck going by at about Mach 7 were all that I had to keep me company. But while I could have counted the number of spectators using my hands and still twiddle my thumbs with the leftover digits, the volunteers were excellent, friendly and relatively plentiful. Only at one point near the end of the race, where a confluence of 10kers, halfers and fullerites met, were the volunteers surprised to see me coming from behind them (I am telling you, I was running all kinds of alone in this race) and it took them about 10 feet to correct me to the right direction.

Trucking down a hill around mile 19, I looked at my watch to do some math. At the pace I was holding (and could very likely hold) I had an outside shot at 3:15 and if I did not get that, could probably lock down that elusive 3:17. I was pleased that in spite of the lack of competition, a tough course and all other things, I was probably going to run pretty close to even splits. Then the damn hills started.

From miles 20-22 there was a series of inclines that just flat-out knocked me on my butt. I was all but done. By mile 23 it was over. I averaged 8:30 miles the last three miles and came in a disappointing 3:22. I did finish sixth overall which helped soothe my ego some but the post-race massage and the wonderful picnic of hot dogs, hamburgers and soda pop soothed everything that much more.

After talking to a few new friends, receiving my age group award medal (a pure ounce of silver shaped like the copper medals given out to all finishers) I headed back to my hosts' place in Reno. A quick shower and a race recap with Sonja and Bryan, I was on the road again to Lake Tahoe. My friend Janice was working in the area and even though I had yet to see my parents once this year, I had now been lucky enough to visit her three times. We explored Lake Tahoe, grabbed lunch and then I turned around again back to Reno. A late pasta dinner later with my hosts and I fell into bed for yet another early wake-up call and all day of traveling.

Marathon 34
Race: Park City Marathon, Park City, UT
Miles from home: 2058.1
890.8 miles raced
471.6 miles to go

Finishing Time: 3:24:10
Place: 17th

From touchdown of my plane to lift-off of my return flight, I did not even get to spend 23 hours in Park City (including running and sleeping). Landing in DC, after the race, I marked my eighty-eighth flight of the year. I am pretty sure I should receive a medal for that. Things I learned:

When you follow a good-looking, World Champion gold-medalist on the speaking dais, you better be funny. Or have a cute dog. I do not have a dog.

If road construction shuts down US 80 going west, your GPS is on the fritz, you are dangerously close to missing your flight, and the only way you know how to get where you are going is US 80 going west, suck it up, use common sense to figure out directions when you have no map, drive it like you stole it, use the sun when you have no idea where you are, and make your pioneering forefathers proud by figuring out where you need to go by just getting there.

A white Jeep Liberty from Advantage Auto Rentals in Salt Lake City goes at least 94 mph.

Ironically, the twenty-three hours I spent in Park City was only my second-shortest stay in this fair city. In 2002, while driving cross-country, I ended up in Park City late at night and had the darnedest time finding a hotel. I soon found out the Sundance Film Festival began the next day, which explained the room shortage.

Landing Saturday afternoon in Salt Lake City, I rented a car (see above Turbo-charged Jeep Liberty: I smell sponsorship! "When your marathon ends and you have to be to the airport on time: Jeep Liberty") and headed to PC, checked into my hotel (which also doubled as the pasta dinner venue and the quaint expo), and gave a ring to PC TV's Ori Hoffer who wanted to do an interview with me about Fiddy2. Staged outside the farmhouse that serves as the halfway point for the race (as well as the logo for the marathon) the interview went very well.

Back to the expo, I laid out my Fiddy2 paraphernalia. I had been given table space to promote Fiddy2 and while nothing fruitful in terms of immediate donations occurred, I got to meet and re-meet many friends. Next up was the pasta dinner.

I was famished. So, I headed into the dinner, planning on vacuum-cleaning some food (of what would be excellently made pasta, salad, rolls and dessert) into my belly and get back to my table to solicit unsuspecting runners for donations. But outside, the race director asked me if I wished to give a short speech about Fiddy2 to those in attendance. Um, is the Pope Catholic?

I realized my impromptu speech was going to follow the keynote speaker, Chris Waddell, a Park City resident who has won countless Paralympics medals in skiing. Worse, he gave an excellent speech, seemed very comfortable doing so and was definitely enjoyed by the crowd. Great. With no speech prepared, I needed to try not to sound like an idiot!

142

I briefly introduced myself, explained Fiddy2 and then opened the floor to questions. I can talk forever about Fiddy2 but I feel somewhat guilty about doing so to people who did not ask for it. However, the crowd seemed to enjoy the give and take and asked some wonderful questions.

After that I headed down to Chris' table to tell him what a great speech he had given and got into an excellent rap session with Chris (a wonderful guy) and with two first-time marathoners from Salt Lake City. And in an irony of ironies, one of these new marathoners was moving to within miles of where I live, at the conclusion of the weekend. After some more chitchat and a few pictures, we finally dispersed and I climbed into bed, spent.

Meeting Ori again at the starting line, I felt a touch of celebrity as he followed me around, with the camera headlight on to illuminate the shot (it was a 6:30 am start.) I also felt a touch unready for the race. Whether it was the short week of rest, the altitude, the early start time or the hard track workout I'd done on Tuesday, I could tell today was going to be a tough race.

The race director counted down from 10 and said, "Wooooooo!"

And away we went.

Like last week, I knew beforehand that both the elevation of the city and the difficulty of the course itself (both perfectly delineated on the website, leaving nothing to guesswork) were going to be a double whammy of a challenge. I did my best to once again run conservatively during the first half and hope that the second half would find me with more energy than I had possessed in my races as of late.

A relatively uneventful first half followed. A few runners told me what I was doing was inspirational and wished me the best of luck. In addition, I chatted with some runners I had run with before, one in Reno the week before and another who had qualified for Boston on his first attempt (how many people hate that guy?) I was enjoying the scenery knowing the difficult hills were yet to come. The open vistas and relatively flat course made it easy to enjoy and all our prayers were answered as the forecasted thunderstorms stayed away.

I was really feeling it this marathon. My usual lethargy for the first 6 miles stretched on and on all the way through the first half of the race. Right along with me was my first time Boston Qualifying guy who said, "I am going to be hurting at the end of this one." I agreed. I could not catch my breath, my legs hurt in places I did not want them to hurt and my mind raced. Had I finally done it? Had I exhausted my tank? Was I going to run over 3:30?

I stopped at the halfway point to apply lubricant to some body parts. For half a minute I thought about the four-mile climb we were about to begin and simply decided to do what I do every week: keep running.

The big hill, normally, would not have been horrible. But cresting a hill at 7,041 feet makes any hill that much more difficult. The promised downhill from the top was helpful, but by the time I got to the top, I could tell the damage had been done. It has always amazed me how true the axiom is that a marathon does not begin until mile 20. Once you have reached that last 10k, your mind starts playing tricks with you. How many people are going to pass me in the last few miles? Did I leave myself enough time to make my flight? Why did I not eat more for breakfast? Where, earlier in the race, you may miss a mile marker because you are in a zone, here you seem to be acutely aware of every tenth of a mile.

Next thing I know a guy and a girl fly by me at mile 25. I hoped they were relay runners, but I could see by the color of their bibs they were not. I wanted to trip them. Instead I tried to match their pace. For half a mile I was right there until I just had nothing left. What is the difference, I thought? Let them finish one person higher. It really does not matter too much to me. (And if you believe I actually think that way, I have some nice property to sell you.)

As my energy fled, one of the wonderful volunteers for the PCM, who I had been introduced to the previous night, appeared (as well as Chris Waddell). I grabbed something out of her outstretched hand that I had requested the night before: hands on springs on a headband. The official symbol of the PCM worn by many of the volunteers, I wanted to cross the finish line wearing these silly things to show my support for one heck of a well-run race. And make no mistake; not being especially pleased with the course had nothing to do with the volunteers, aid stations or anything else about the race.

I crossed the line in 3:24:10, sixteenth overall and fifth in my age group (so darn annoying that my age group is that competitive!); I gave my 'head-hands' a high five and basked in the glory of yet another marathon completed. While the mystery may be gone, as any marathoner will tell you, the race still is 26.2 miles long. So much can happen during that distance. In fact, a quote from Emil Zapata that Chris used at the pasta dinner sums up my feelings perfectly: "If you want to win something, run 100 meters. If you want to experience something, run a marathon."

A kind announcer mentioned Fiddy2 and I received a great deal of congrats from, what I hope, are many new friends. Knowing my time was limited, I reluctantly said goodbye to everyone, grabbed some liquids and food, hobbled up the hill to my car, dashed to my hotel, showered, explored all of SLC and finally got onto my flight. Sleeping in my own bed Saturday night and waking up under my own volition whenever the heck I wanted to for about only the third Sunday this year made the rush worth the effort.

32

I Heart Downhill

Marathon 35
Race: New Mexico Marathon, Albuquerque, NM
Miles from home: 1881.3
917 miles raced
445.4 miles to go

Finishing Time: 3:13:31
Place: 11th

In the departure lounge for my flight out of D.C. the ground attendant made this announcement: "All those in rows 1-2 have boarded. Everyone else: come on up!" You should have seen the rush.

It was great to meet new friends whom you have "known" for a while, and to see old friends is the ideal way to spend 23 hours in Albuquerque. Especially when they are good looking.

This week brought to a close 12 straight weeks of flying all over the country and then some. I raced in Colorado twice, Oregon, Washington, Maine, Nova Scotia, California, Alaska, Wisconsin, Nevada, Utah and New Mexico.

The first eight miles was a series of hills but none were tremendously awful or tremendously helpful. However, even though I knew I was mostly running uphill until this point, I was shocked to see my time at mile 8. I had not run a slower first eight miles this year, discounting Leadville. (For the most part, Leadville never figures into my calculations for this entire year.) I think running in the pitch black was the main culprit. From my experience, it is much more difficult to keep a solid pace when it is dark outside.

But I took heart in knowing that after these eight miles I had what I thought was a 4-mile downhill to make up some time. And unlike some recent marathons these downhills did not come at a point where I would be too tired to take advantage of them.

When I hit mile 16 I realized I had not run a faster 16 miles this year. How the heck did that happen? Many times up to this point it had only taken me 55-56 minutes to traverse the first eight miles of the course. While I did the best I could to stave off worries of a horrible time, I do admit being three minutes slower than usual gave me a scare. But then what I thought was a 4-mile downhill, turned into a 7-mile downhill. It had been a long time since I have run that fast, that late in a race. I was elated.

And while I had passed six runners on this downhill, I thoroughly expected them all to catch me during the remaining ten miles. I know my strengths and after pushing it so hard here, was sure I would eventually falter. I had been tired, sore and deflated as of late. The year was getting to me. Heck, I had set my personal best for the year nearly four months prior in Delaware. I shouldn't be too hard on myself for slowing a little as the year ended, right? It only makes sense.

I would be remiss if I did not mention my good hometown friend Damon who was my host, chauffeur and sustenance provider during the race. Stopping every two miles or so to see how I was doing, he also provided me with words of encouragement greatly needed on this sparsely-spectated course.

As I have said before with other early start marathons, I don't blame spectators for not showing up at 5:30 am. But a friendly face every few miles helps one forget some of the unpleasantries during a race.

With a packet of Gu handed to me right before the turn off the highway at mile 17, I shot past a few half-marathon walkers onto a nice little bike/running path. (God love ya for exercising, but you cannot walk four abreast, people. You simply cannot.) I was eyeing the only guy who had passed me on the downhills (rat bastard.) He happened to be a very fit, intricately tattooed man who I would never call "rat bastard" to his face. I was wondering if he would be able to pull me to the finish. I was feeling better than I thought I would be and when the Gu kicked in I got a little energy boost. I hoped I would not have to out sprint him to the finish because, well, I was tired.

But, as often happens in a marathon, just one step, one falter of a runner in front of you, something almost unseen to the naked eye, can give you an extra energy boost and a killer instinct. I saw Tat Man drop a shoulder, or hesitate on a step, or something and I just knew he was toast. So I took off, flew past him and never saw him again.

Around mile 21 one of the guys I'd passed at mile 16 caught up to me. I could tell he was fresher than I but decided to hang with him to the end. We spoke for a few seconds and he asked, "Are you the guy who..."

"Yes," I interrupted. "You going to take pity on me and let me beat you?"

He smirked. "Fat chance. Good luck on all your races!" and started to pull away.

Mile 24 approached and I still had him in my sights somewhere about 45 seconds ahead of me. I could not believe how fast I was running. About a mile back I'd seen Damon for the last time and told him, "I am cruising. But I am tired. See you at the end." I reached down deep for the energy to pass Smirky Guy. But I did not have it this time. He continued to pull away. My energy was rapidly slipping but I had a goal in mind. I wanted to set a Fiddy2 PR.

The downhills had given me the chance to set this new personal best for the year and I was not going to let them go to waste. Hopes for a 3:10 or a 3:11 passed by but I still had a shot for a 3:12. Nearing the last mile I was shocked to see that as hard as I had pushed, I had not run any faster. I was sure I had run a 7:20 or 7:30 mile but instead but clocked in at 7:45. Little things like that just crush you. I was not going to make 3:12.

I made one turn, and then another, and then finally one more and I could see the finish line ahead. The new old friends were both waiting for me next to the chutes as I sprinted down the line. (Way to go Brandy on your half-marathon! Good luck Molly next week at Imogene Pass!) Damon was there as well and had his camera poised to snap a shot.

I crossed the line in 3:13:31. Good enough for 11th overall and while not a "new" minute, good enough for my best time so far for the year. In my 35th marathon of the year (and 47th lifetime marathon) I had run the eighth fastest time of my life.

The question of whether running at elevation affects me has been settled. It does. But not nearly as much as hills or heat. On two separate courses this year, both over a mile high, but with little overall elevation gain, I have run a 3:13 and a 3:16.

While I hoped I would be able to do the same thing the next weekend in Erie, I only cared about one thing: I would see my family for the first time in 2006.

33

For My Family

Marathon 36
Race: Presque Isle Marathon, Erie, PA
Miles from home: 357.9 (or 44 from my parents' house)
943.2 miles raced
419.2 miles to go

Finishing Time: 3:10:17
Place: 19th

I lived in Erie for over a year and routinely had bad races here for no reason at all. This was the fourth marathon I had ever run twice, and while the course had changed slightly due to construction, it was nice to know what to expect. My mom wears some of the brightest colors imaginable and I loved it because it was so easy to spot her. She also sat on the back of my convertible like she was a prom queen, while Anne drove the course, wearing a Fiddy2 placard a co-worker had once made for me, waving to everyone on the course and yelling "Go Fiddy2!"

I have been very inefficient in my side quest to knock out as many states as possible during Fiddy2 (mostly because of money concerns) making this the 3rd Pennsylvania marathon I have run in my life with two more to go this year: Johnstown and Philly.

150

This weekend marked the first time in 2006 that I was able to spend time with my parents. In order to make the most of it, I took an extra day off of work so I could actually enjoy the time at "home", instead of rushing around like usual. And, having brought my PR Chick Anne with me to enjoy the festivities, I did more sightseeing in my own hometown than I have almost anywhere else this year.

After dinner with the folks, we realized that a high school football game was just about to start. We hurried over to Carter Field, where I recounted to Anne some great football memories as we watched the Titusville Rockets lambaste the Franklin Knights 26-0. I also chatted with many people I knew but the caboose was calling our names so we hit the hay.

Saturday was more of the same as I enjoyed my parents' company and showed Anne the wonder that is a town where five-bedroom 3-story homes go for $150,000. Then time for an early bedtime because while the 7:30 am start was not all that early, I still needed to pick up my race packet and bib number.

My mother and Anne rode up to Erie with me. It was the first time my mother would see me run a marathon. At the start, my mom's brother and sister and my uncle's girlfriend all were waiting to cheer me on. This was unexpected and made my heart swell. As I have mentioned, my marathoning is dedicated to my grandparents. And this race was being run on Grandparent's Day.

At the start, I ran into my good friend David Terrill. Dave was running this race to honor his daughter who is fighting overseas in the army. His goal was to run a 2:58, which was rather lofty given his PR of 3:04. However, I could hear in his voice and see in his eyes that little was going to stop him.

Also, I saw my friend Holly who had never run a marathon until she lost the use of her legs in an accident, and has since completed several in a wheelchair. Unfortunately, I did not get to talk to her and when I shouted out her name at the beginning of the race the cheers drowned me out.

I first saw my family around mile six. I later learned that my aunt said to Anne, "See Dane run! He doesn't look tired at all!" If she only knew that you sure as heck better not look tired at mile six, she might have laughed as much as I did when I was told what she had said. But she may have been right, as I felt great. I knew I was going fast. The course is flat and forgiving and if you keep your head about you can be super fast and still save energy. In fact, although I felt like I was holding back a bit I still rocketed out to sub 7 minute/mile pace.

I slowed for the next few miles but I was still feeling good. Very good, in fact. Bridge construction caused a slight deviation from the normal course. This mile-long jaunt through the woods was a nice mental and visual break from the flatness of the rest of the race. The route was well marked by the marathon crew but you had to keep alert as it was run on some uneven concrete slabs. In addition, what wind was on the course seemed to be a little stiffer here than anywhere else.

Dan, a former co-worker in Erie, had made it out to the race and shuttled back and forth with my parents to help cheer. Bringing me the depth charge sized Gatorade, his moral support was just as greatly appreciated. I saw Dan, Anne and my mom at mile 12 and then my aunt at the halfway point. She was jumping around like she knew someone famous.

When I hit mile 16 I realized I had not run a faster sixteen miles this year. If that seems like a quote from the previous week's race, that is because it is. I just cut and pasted it here because, well, this was now the fastest I have ever hit the 16-mile marker. In fact, I had actually sped up from the halfway point to here and had visions of not only a Fiddy2 PR but also an overall PR.

As I rounded the turn at 16, my uncle drove up. He told me I was looking good – for a Penn Stater. I pretended I did not see him and mimed tossing my water cup on his University of Pittsburgh t-shirt. But I figured he already knew that the University of Pittsburgh has not been relevant in any real college football discussion since, well, I think when the Mayflower landed. Give or take.

Instead, I told him today was for Gramma and Grandpa (his parents).

I have been doing this long enough to know how you feel at mile sixteen means relatively little. And sure enough around mile 18.5, I saw my mile times dip precipitously. More angry than tired at this slip when I was still pushing, I tried picking it up. Mom and Anne gave me a Propel at mile 19 and I took the whole bottle. About half a mile later I felt refreshed.

152

But as we crossed once again into the renovated section (the marathon was two loops of a half marathon course), I heard footsteps. In quick succession a woman and two guys passed me. But it was not about placement today. Today was about time. I knew there was a Gu packet waiting for me at mile 22. Push, Dane.

I burst out of the woods, grabbed the Gu, swigged down some water and took a 10 second walk break. Those who had passed me in the woods were even further ahead now. Rick, a chap I had met online and at the race start came into sight. I knew he was trying to qualify for Boston and his previous best was a 3:28. I knew he would be close to this at this pace but was going to be in trouble unless he picked it up. I also knew just being close would not make him feel good about a huge drop in his PR if he missed Boston. So I began to work on catching him. In the meantime, two women passed me in quick succession. (I would later learn that this turned into a showdown as only one second separated the winner and second place. Go girls!)

With 2 miles left I caught Rick.

"Am I going to make it?" he asked me.

"Not at this pace. Come on!" We increased our turnover pace and cranked out two 7:15ish miles. We hit the 26-mile marker at 3:08. I know it only takes me about 1:30 to do that last .2. Even though it had been established in conversation at mile four that he was in my age group, I eased up a smidgen, watched him turn on the jets and fly in to a 3:10:04. Way to go Rick!

I sauntered into the finish line at 3:10:17 with both hands pointing up to Gramma and Grandpa. I was so happy I did not even hear the announcer saying wondrous things about Fiddy2.

I had garnered my Fiddy2 PR, my fifth fastest time ever and qualified for Boston in my 36th marathon in one year. Greeted by a slew of family and friends I can say that I have not had a happier moment this year.

Top that off with a wonderful age group award, finding out that not only had David run a sub 3 hour marathon but took third overall with a 2:54 (holy crap!) and the Erie Runners Club presentation of an extraordinarily generous check for L'Arche Mobile and I have to say I had a good weekend.

I hope my grandparents were proud.

34

Inspiration Lends Its Jersey

Marathon 37

Race: Rochester Marathon, Rochester, NY
Miles from home: 399.1
969.4 miles raced
393 miles to go

Finishing Time: 3:16:20
Place: 18th

As early as February I had been planning bits and pieces of this race. One piece I did not plan, that was absolutely wonderful, was seeing my friend Nathalie. In her first half marathon ever she placed second overall in the Master's women!

Hearken back with me my friends to late February in Tampa. I was visiting my brother and preparing for the eighth marathon of the year and I spied video on television about a high school kid on a Rochester, NY basketball team who had made quite a stir. Actually, he was the manager for the basketball team and it was not until the final game of his senior year that this young guy, Jason McElwain, even put on a jersey. This was done without any real intention of letting him play, but rather to reward his hard work and endless spirit as a manager. Jason, who happens to be autistic, made huge waves that night. During what was turning into a blow out, the coach inserted Jason into the game. Jason missed his first two shots. Then, catching fire, Jason followed up his misses with six straight 3-pointers, including one at the buzzer to send the local high school into hysterics.

As I watched the screen my eyes caught something truly cool: Jason's basketball jersey happened to be 52. It is not surprising that I see this number everywhere and since I would be running the marathon in Rochester, I decided to do something to honor Jason.

Over the next few months, I found Jason had become quite a celebrity and it was pretty difficult to get in touch with him. Finally making contacting, I learned that my plan to run the last half-mile with Jason would not be possible. On the day of the race in his hometown, he would be where I live; In DC giving a speech.

However, one aspect of my plan worked out wonderfully: to run the entire race wearing Jason's basketball jersey. We met Saturday night prior to the race and Jason, his wonderful father and I spoke for a few minutes. Jason is just a great kid. When no-talent hacks can sign contracts for millions of dollars to "sing", and real heroes like firefighters and policeman often have to take a second job just to make ends meet, I am pulling for Jason to continue to inspire others, as he has already done me, for a long time to come.

The morning broke with a dense fog. Temperatures promised to reach into the 80s so we all hoped this fog would stay for quite some time. Our hopes were in vain.

Opening up with a steady 5-mile downhill (which was far steeper than I thought it was going to be) I was happy to keep myself in check as the temps soared. Unfortunately, while inspirational, the basketball jersey was far from lightweight and was soaking up my sweat like a sponge. In addition, the jersey was so long I had doubled it up and pinned it lest it hang down to my knees.

I hit mile 8 in a time only slightly slower than last week. Still, I knew there were some uphills to battle later and I was already feeling the sun's effects.

"Almost halfway there!" is not inspirational. Nevertheless, I hit the halfway point just two minutes off my pace from the previous week and still felt relatively good. Running along the Erie Canal provided some wonderful views of homes I will never be able to afford, while a breeze off of the canal helped battle the sun overhead.

I spoke to a few runners who were shocked that I was not running New York City's marathon. I told them I had not gained entry through the lottery and to this point had received no positive answer from the marathon organizers.

The next few miles were lined with spectators and a great many Fleet Feet team members. A nice woman I met the night before saw my jersey, turned around to these teens and yelled, "A marathon every week for the whole year!"

They went ballistic. I only had one more hill at mile 18, and this little demonstration gave me an energy boost. But the one hill turned into a series of small, but continuous hills. The beautiful bike path along the canal made for an enjoyable run, but I was just not expecting the hills. Starting at mile 22, my miles continued to get slower and slower and nothing I did changed that. The jersey was heavy, I was hot, and I just wanted to finish.

Nathalie would be done with her half and Anne would be working her magic to get the announcer to talk about Jason's jersey. The finishing area of the minor league baseball team, the Rochester Redwings, loomed ahead. Unfortunately, in order to complete the race, I had to do a complete loop around the stadium and then once inside the stadium had to run the entire length of the warming track and then down the third base line. By this last stretch I was really hurting. But the cheers for the finishers from hundreds sitting in the stands lifted my spirits and I crossed the line in...yet another 3:16. I am beginning to think I should get that tattooed somewhere.

Jason McElwain, the autistic basketball player who wowed all with a 3-point barrage in his final high school game, lent his #52 jersey to Dane to wear during the Rochester Marathon.

35

Time Begins to Fade Away

Marathon 38
Race: Quad Cities Marathon, Moline, IL
Miles from home: 843.4
995.6 miles raced
366.8 miles to go

Finishing Time: 3:12:25
Place: 24th

This was my 50th lifetime marathon and 46th since the start of 2004. I got the chance to meet and mingle with Patti Catalano Dillon, the first woman to run sub 2:31, 2:30, 2:29 and 2:28 in a marathon. The winner's time for this race of 2:16:36 was the fastest winner's time of any marathon I have raced this year. And I surpassed 100 flights for the year, touching down in D.C. Sunday night with #102.

What a wonderful time I had in the Quad Cities. Separated by the Mississippi River, these four cities, two abreast on either side of the river, offered a small town feel. You are treated like a king (or queen) but still receive all the perks of a big race.

I was once again taken by surprise when the race director asked me to give a short speech about Fiddy2 at the pasta dinner. (Of course, I should not be too surprised by the race director Joe Moreno. An affable gentleman, Joe is so intent on making sure that his race is run correctly, that in 2005, when a train threatened to cut off runners, he blocked its path with his truck! You cannot make this stuff up.)

So I once again spun the yarn of Fiddy2 to a group of runners eating their Saturday night spaghetti. The applause was heartfelt and made me feel warm inside. After every one of these speeches, I always wished I could have spoken longer and more often.

I listened to Patti Catalano's wonderful story of achieving things that she never thought possible. I was able to enjoy this speech all the more as I was very relaxed after a massage from my new friend/masseuse/chauffeur for the weekend, Laurel. One of the official masseuses for the marathon, Laurel also treated me to a guided tour of the John Deere factory. Here I saw my friend and fellow runner, Jack. Jack loves being the biggest tourist possible everywhere he goes. He was taking pictures of farm equipment, and slides about farm equipment, and signs describing the slides about the farm equipment, etc. I teased him mercilessly.

After this tour I grabbed a bite to eat at a local sub shop called the Hungry Hobo. I was so taken by their logo that I asked the manager if I could have one of the Hungry Hobo visors that the employees were wearing. When she acquiesced, I told Laurel I was damn sure wearing that visor the next day in the race.

After a sleep that went by too fast, the morning broke and it was time for the 38th consecutive week of lubing up all the body parts which might chafe, fueling the body for the next three-plus hours of running and heading out. Just another Sunday morning in 2006 for Dane.

While my time splits were almost identical to the previous week's first few miles, I could tell I was in for a much faster run. Around mile two, I heard a guy behind me say: "Dane?" Lo and behold I was running with Mike, with whom I had been emailing for months. He told me he would be at the race but his description of "blue hat, blue shirt and black shorts" was probably the same description given by seventeen other people that morning. Luckily, he found me (while I'd like to think it is my winning personality that led him to me, I am all but assured it was my ears) and we spent the next few miles running together. Mike said he had just ran a marathon two weeks prior and would be happy with a 3:20 on this day.

A full two minutes faster than last week proved how much a huge basketball jersey in hot weather can slow one down. I received a little kick right before the half when a local high school band began playing Rock and Roll Part 2 (better known as the "Hey Song"). They hit the "Hey!" part right after I went by and I threw my hands in the air for the first two and then did a little Charlie Chaplin-type heel click on the third. I overheard a snippet of conversation:

Flutist: "Isn't this mile thirteen?"

Band Director: "Yeah. Just down that hill is halfway."

Flutist: "He has far too much energy."

Perhaps I did, but it did not stop the Pavlovian response of " LET'S. GO. PSU!" from coming out of my mouth after that final "Hey!" I had pulled away from Mike but knew he was not too far behind. I had also seen Jack in one of the out and back parts and he was a lot closer to me than expected. I wondered if he was going to set a PR today. I was pretty sure his PR was a 3:26. (Jack is old, give him some credit. Kidding.)

Four minutes faster than last week and still feeling good. In an attempt to make each mile split look good in my mind, I would push very hard when I saw each mile marker. Of course, pushing so hard would make my energy ebb a little soon after, but these were the games I had to play.

Here, I would like to note a really nice touch by the Quad Cities marathon people. Tethered to each mile marker were large balloons attached to a lengthy piece of string. I could see the mile markers from about 90 seconds away and it helped me push. I wish more races would do something similar.

I was still holding steady at approximately 4 minutes faster than the previous week. I knew I would finish in a good time. Coming off a bridge at mile 20, I noticed a thin runner sprinting back at me and realized this was the leader. He was nearly six miles ahead of me and I was hardly slacking. Wow. I realized why many runners, who might be in the middle of the pack, could get demoralized when runners pass them in similar situations.

At the turn-around heading back, I once again saw Jack far sooner than I expected. He was looking great and I was excited for him. And since I did not want him to catch me, it also gave me a kick in the butt! So I dialed up my pace and passed a few runners who had passed me in the last few miles. I then saw Laurel coming the opposite direction. She was competing in her third marathon, and definitely looked tired. I guess massaging elite runners the day before had taken its toll on her. In addition, the sun had broken through and the weather was getting warmer by the minute. Not helpful.

It might be possible to get a 3:11, but honestly, I was beat. Earlier in the week, when asked what time I thought I might get, I had thrown out the number: 3:12. So, I decided to stick to that and cruised in to the announcer yelling, "Here comes Dane Rausch...Roshen...Roochen...from Arlington, Virginia!" It is really not that hard a name but an "A" for effort goes to the announcer. Actually that grade goes to all the volunteers and spectators at this race. It is clear that they take great pride in putting on a wonderful event. They succeeded.

I took a big lumberjack step on the finisher's mat to signify I had arrived and my time read 3:12:25. Good enough only for 34th overall (I told you this was a strong field) but my second fastest time of the year. In fact, three of the four races I ran in September were the fastest I had run all year. Maybe I was getting stronger, contrary to what many thought.

Mike ran a stellar 3:18, far faster than what he was hoping for on the day; Jack crushed his personal best by close to 4 minutes in running a 3:22 and Laurel, who got hit with some stomach issues in the last 10k, gutted out a fine performance given the circumstances.

I had a chance to once again thank so many of the volunteers at the end of the race and then had the pleasure of riding to the airport with some of the elite Ethiopians. They were all very nice gentlemen. Who can beat me by like a friggin hour.

Marathon 39
Race: Johnstown Marathon, Johnstown, PA
Miles from home: 177.1
1021.8 miles raced
340.6 miles to go

Finishing Time: 3:05:10
Place: 7th

My Race:

- If Fiddy2 were a deck of cards, I just completed three suits.
- Double check the time of the football game you are going to attend.
- I swear the sheep bleating at us was saying: "WE ARE!" so we bleated back "PENN STATE!"

At the beginning of the year, it seemed my tradition of attending at least one home Penn State game for the past thirteen years was in jeopardy. As if the logistics of planning Fiddy2 were not daunting enough, now I was praying for a home PSU game within good traveling distance of a marathon. As luck would have it, one weekend provided such a confluence of factors. With the Johnstown Marathon just a short two-hour drive away from Penn State, I was excited beyond words. I asked Anne to join me so she could see a real college football game (she had been to a Pitt game a few weeks ago and, well, that just is not football.)

A bright and early start got us to PSU before the noon game. There wasn't much traffic. Then I realized why it had been so easy: the game did not start until 3:30. Whoops. But this actually worked to our advantage as we toured the campus and I got to see how much had changed. Then it was off to the game!

PSU prevailed 33-7. After sitting in the cold rain at the game, the warm comfort of my car made us both rather drowsy. Anne slept while I listened to the recap of the game and soon we were in Johnstown. A quick late dinner at Perkins led to a relatively early bedtime and sweet dreams. I slept better than I have in quite some time.

With race day upon us, we headed into Johnstown. Let us just say that without the kind help of some strangers there would have been no way we would have found the start of the race. On top of the Johnstown Incline, some kind people actually led us to the top (and then later, as Anne told me, drove at least 15 miles from their home to meet Anne at mile 22 in an effort to see how I was doing; and then turned around and went back home.) Thank you very much.

In spite of my time, I did not feel good for the first 8 miles. If I was going to have a decent day I was really going to have to work at it. The fact that this was the fastest eight miles of the year meant little to me as I knew the two-mile hill starting at mile 5 aided in bringing my time this low. Not fully knowing what the rest of the course held in store for me I did not run this downhill all-out.

At Mile 10 I visited a porta-potty. I came out feeling much better and spent the next two miles trying to track down the guy who I had been running with before my stop. (The "stop" took over 90 seconds). I knew Todd was an ultra-marathoner and with his personal best of 2:57 in a marathon, I hoped he could pace me. Problem was I needed to catch him. He had run this race before and possessed an intimate knowledge of what came ahead; I needed to use his memory.

As Anne progressed on the course, was shadowed by the ultra-marathoner's family, Todd and I ran down some very forgiving downhills, before hitting a nice solid one-mile uphill. We were both shocked when we ran this mile in 7:09. Soon my time at the half blew me away, especially given bathroom break and the general feeling of malaise.

By now, Todd and I had separated from everyone else on the course. No one was in sight in front of us and we were now running alone. After crossing a bridge and traversing up another tough hill, Todd told me that it was smooth sailing from here on out (at least for downhill lovers like me). But the thing is, God himself could appear and tell me the race course will favor me the rest of the way and I would still say: "Well, me and my friend Thomas will just see for ourselves. But thanks, God. Thomas has this doubting problem. We are working on it."

I simply made a noise agreeing with what Todd had said.

Around mile 18, Todd reached to grab a drink from his son and missed the handle. I heard him slow down to retrieve it but having just started up another hill, I could not afford to stop and wait. So I pressed on, fully expecting him to catch me.

It was then that a wonderful sight appeared in front of me: a huge downhill. Todd had not lied. Even though I kept waiting for another uphill to appear to throw me off, four more miles passed almost all downhill.

I looked at my watch; if I could get to mile 19 at my current pace, I could average 8-minute miles the rest of the way and run my fastest time of Fiddy2. I could not believe that was all I had to average, so I spent the next mile re-working the math in my head. Anne stopped here and there to see if I needed anything. However aside from swigs of Gatorade (and very few other drinks from the plentiful volunteers on this rural course) I had taken in no sustenance all day long. No Gu, no nothing. What was going on?

I realized something special was going to happen if I just kept my head and did not get injured running too hard. At mile 24, when some cute girls sang along to a stereo playing Poison's "Talk Dirty To Me" I was in heaven (mostly from my time, but the girls helped). My watch was not lying.

I crossed a bridge. I had to run past the stadium where the race ended, travel a few more blocks before turning around. Down a few blocks, turn right and come back towards the stadium. I was very happy. I somehow ran two consecutive 7:05 miles without much effort and I came to the last .2 of a mile. As someone with a walkie-talkie radioed my number to the press box, someone shouted my name over the loudspeaker. I entered the stadium smiling broadly.

I was handed my medal and received a big hug from a dumbfounded Anne. At the Albuquerque Marathon I had given an interview to NPR after the race where I sounded like I was on death's door. For all my friends and family who were worried, I could only have wished that they saw me here. I was completely and utterly not tired. I was not sore, I was not winded, and I was not even hungry. Somehow I had knocked off 2 minutes from my best time ever and I felt like I had only run 4 miles.

Todd came in behind me and while I failed to catch his time, I was able to tell him his leadership earlier on had been paramount to my success. I hugged him but made sure to give him that one hard pat on the back that guys give each other to remain masculine.

I then gathered up my things, grabbed my second place age group award and left. I had hurry back to D.C. The Bears were going to be on national TV and as a rabid Chicago fan, raised in Steeler country, now living in Redskins land, you do what it takes to watch their games.

36

Beneath the Memorials

Marathon 40
Race: Mt. Rushmore Marathon, Rapid City, SD
Miles from home: 1616.9
1048 miles raced
314.4 miles to go

Finishing Time: 3:13:32
Place: 3rd

This was my 52nd lifetime marathon. In the week after I was featured in Sports Illustrated, I had one of my worst total fundraising weeks this year. Publicity obviously is not correlated to donations. At least not for me.

Going into this weekend, I knew I was taking part in an interesting race. Technically, two separate marathons were going to be run in essentially the same area at virtually the same time. Called the Mount Rushmore/Crazy Horse Marathon, one course begins in the shadows of Mt. Rushmore and the other, well, you guessed it, begins underneath the unfinished Crazy Horse Monument. One of the sad states of our nation today is how exorbitant amounts of money are spent in some areas (running for political office comes to mind) and the construction of a wonderful testament to this Native American moves along at a snail's pace, not for lack of labor but for the lack of funds.

A few days before the race I looked at the course elevation profiles. As chancy as these elevations profiles can be for accuracy, I still like to know what is in store for me. On the other hand, I often do not really have the opportunity to check out the courses too far in advance. From what I could tell, Mt. Rushmore (MR) began with a series of rolling hills for its first half. The Crazy Horse Marathon (CH) had what appeared to be a massive downhill for the first 11 miles or so. After that, the courses followed the same course until the end.

While the prize money for this race was, this year, on the CH half-marathon and the MR full marathon, being a lover of downhills, I opted for the CH course. I called the race director, who made the switch for me. While it cost me my 52 bib number I felt the greater need of saving my legs for the last 12 marathons of the year was well worth that small sacrifice.

I flew in the day before the race, and had little time to acclimate to the 5,000 plus elevation. I found out that this might not be my day. The first 5k or so contained a few surprising uphills that quickly skewed my time upward and put any hopes of running a PR out of reach. It is amazing how in three miles you more or less know whether your goose is cooked. However, I hoped the promised downhill would bring that time down and I could salvage the race. (Many of us were shocked by the size of the uphills at the start, as we twice traversed a parking lot with some big hills in it.)

I simply was not feeling it. The downhill we eventually got to was on the Michelson Trail which is a soft and forgiving dirt trail that many runners like. Call me crazy, but I like hard road better. Nevertheless, the trail was indeed constantly downhill but was far more gentle than I imagined it would be. I will, of course, take any downhill over any uphill any day, but this was not going to be the steep decline I would have liked. With the added difficulty of the elevation (topping out at just under 6,000 feet) and thinner air, I decided to settle in and make sure I ran under 3:20.

Around mile 10 a woman came out of nowhere to my right and was quickly running side-by-side with me. Sporting the bib number "1" I assumed she was one of the 5k frontrunners. (There were numerous events being held this weekend.). However, I soon realized she was the lead female runner of the MR marathon and where she had joined in was where they all would be joining in. So, for the next three miles I kept her right in front of me and used her as a pacer. Nothing wrong with using a pretty girl as motivation, right? I hit the halfway point a few minutes faster than I thought I was going to and

I credit Nikki for this effort. To show what a small world running can be, this Rapid City resident had belonged to my running club in D.C. just a short time before I joined.

This is where the fun began. I am, of course, completely joking.

As soon as we left the halfway point in Hill City and passed one of the very few places where there were any spectators that were not deer (and in one place I swear I saw a cougar), we began a super steep uphill. Keeping my pacer in sight helped me power through them even though there were times when I wanted to quit. Now, do not read too greatly into that. Usually, at least once in every race, I have this thought of bagging it, walking off the course and going home. Normally, it is a passing one that never reappears and as usual, it left me quickly.

However, this thought first appeared on race day not only because of the hills I was climbing but also because there were relatively few mile markers. Gale force winds during the night had blown many of them away. While the race director had woken up even earlier than usual to try to remedy this situation, I would go three miles (or more sometimes) without seeing one. Now, mile markers are essential in helping me pass over small psychological barriers when I am just not feeling it.

Luckily for me, right when I needed it most, a marathon runner who had long ago disappeared from my sight reappeared in front of me. As Nikki disappeared into the distance, I focused on this new target. (Incidentally, in spite of not feeling too hot I was running surprisingly fast uphill mile splits.)

On every uphill I would catch up to my prey and every downhill he would pull further away. I am not used to being the stronger uphill and weaker downhill runner, so this was a new experience for me. As we ventured off of the highway and back onto some trails into some heavily wooded areas around mile 21, he disappeared. He had about a 50-meter lead on me, I figured perhaps I had missed a turn. My head was on a swivel from left to right and I finally spotted him off to my right answering a little call from nature. I decided that with nothing but downhill the rest of the way and based on the running he had done previously, he was definitely going to be able to catch me after his "break" was over. But damn it, he was going to work for it. So for the next two miles, I pushed it even harder than I had at any point in the race. Then

I realized how hungry I was. And then I realized I had drunk next to nothing during the whole race.

What was going on? In Johnstown the week before, I had done virtually the same thing. This seemed to go against everything I had read and also personally experienced about marathon running. I only had time to think about this for a few minutes before I heard footsteps.

Poopie von FastDownhiller had caught me. Oh well. I had held him off for a few miles and even though I really wanted to beat him (for reasons to become clear very soon) I knew I did not have it in me. So, I let him go. Then, within the next mile or so, two more guys passed me. But from their bibs I could see they were running the MR course and therefore their times would not factor into my overall place. (May I add this was a unique and interesting idea? While the overall logistics need a little tweaking this could become a destination marathon.)

A few more miles on the trail spit us back out into Hill City's streets. I rounded a bend into the home stretch in the downtown area. A nice crowd had gathered at the finish line but what had grabbed my attention was the time. My watch said 3:13 something and the race clock said 3:15. What happened to my watch? And was I going to run another damn 3:16? Well the answer to those questions is "Nothing" and "No." I found out later the displayed time was for those who were running the MR marathon. My watch was correct and 3:13:32 was my time. 3:13 was becoming my new 3:16.

Now, why did I want to kick it in so bad and why am I glad that I did not? Well, to answer those in reverse order, the guy in front of me was one place back from what I thought he was. And I am happy I did not kick it in as I would have been very disappointed to know that I put in all that extra effort and not placed where I thought I was going to be.

You see, with my effort on this day I nailed my second bronze place of the year. And the prize for third place overall was a 25 pound hunk of granite hewed from the Black Hills. Other than the hernia I risked lugging it through the airport, I could not have been happier with my award. When I found out later that fourth place was 20 minutes behind me, I was even more pleased.

Dane races through the beauty of the Black Hills of the Crazy Horse
Marathon to a 3rd place overall.

37

Pacing Part Two

Marathon 41
Race: Des Moines Marathon, Des Moines, Iowa
Miles from home: 1616.9
1074.2 miles raced
288.2 miles to race

Finishing Time: 3:10:12
Place: 57th

I found out on Friday before the race that I would be able to run the NYC Marathon. Because of their assistance in helping me do so, I would honor New York's Fire Departments by wearing a FD NY cap for the marathon. At this point it had begun to hit me how few marathons I had left this year and how much still could go massively awry.

Often I am asked if I am excited about the upcoming marathon. Unfortunately, I am mostly a downer when I answer, something about how it is impossible to be excited when there are so many variables beyond my control. Flying into Des Moines Friday night (late by the way: thank you airlines!) I at least was able to rest easy knowing I was in the city where I would be running on Sunday.

As the end of the year drew close, and I made it perfectly clear I was not just running 52 marathons but one every weekend, the desire, nay, necessity to make sure that this feat would continue to happen increased every seven days. I wonder how the two runners who had done this before me handled the pressure. Was there even any pressure since they weren't advertising their efforts? Where did those runners do a marathon on Christmas weekend? Did they do Leadville (seemingly the only marathon in America the first weekend of July)? Were they working a job? Were they sponsored?

These unanswered questions helped me keep my mind off the fact that heading to Des Moines, I still had as many marathons left to run as I had run in my entire life coming into 2006.

However, when a member of the race committee wearing a Fiddy2 shirt greeted me heartily at the airport in Des Moines, I smiled. It was much easier to focus on the great things in store for me. For one, I knew I was presenting the race director with a signed photo that he had asked for and hoped he would appreciate how thankful I was for his Iowan hospitality.

At the expo, I was given the chance to do a Q&A about Fiddy2 over the PA system. I saw Patti Dillon again and met her incredibly well mannered son. Browsing the expo, I saw pace groups for this marathon were being offered and the race organizers were seeking pace group leaders. With a 3:10 group glaring at me, I thought about leading that pace group. However, I had only run 3:10 or below twice this year and seven times total so I was uneasy about my ability to do so. But I figured this was my way of paying back the karma gods and somehow thanking that pacesetter who had helped me qualify for Boston back in January in 2005.

So, in spite of the enormous pressure involved, I decided I would do it. I was given a bright yellow singlet and a three-foot dowel rod to carry with a sign declaring I was the 3:10 Pace Group Leader. I was told since I also had a "3:10" on the back of my singlet as well, I only needed to hold the sign for the first few miles. Then I was invited to meet the rest of the pacesetters at dinner later on which I thoroughly enjoyed. I got back to the hotel just in time to watch both the Mets and Penn State lose games. This did not bode well for my run. Hoping nothing else bad would happen, I headed to bed.

The alarm rang and I rushed out into the brisk morning air. My friend Laurel met me, running in her second marathon in less than a month; she was excited. She then noticed my bright singlet and handed me a pair of gloves that matched it. For some reason, not only did she have two pairs of gloves but she had bright yellow ones. I did not ask why.

I received a very nice introduction at the start at the race over the PA systems. Some random runner commented, "That guy is running his forty-first marathon this year!"

That prompted me to reply, "I heard he's a jerk. But stunningly handsome!"

The gun cracked and away we went.

The first 10k was rolling hills. I wanted to make sure to keep my group (at least 30 strong at the beginning) reserved and strong for the supposedly flat rest of the race. One chap who wanted to run a 3:10, took off like a shot near mile 2. This was only his second marathon; I was hoping he knew what he was doing.

After the first six miles of hills, we ran on some suburban streets lined with trees which would have effectively blocked any sun if there had been any. After that we burst into Drake University stadium, home of the famous Drake Relays. Here we were treated to visions of ourselves on the JumboTron up above. On a time delay of about 40 seconds, a camera caught us as we entered the backstretch of the track, which allowed us to see ourselves when we left the stadium. I am even uglier 20 feet tall.

The first miles were relatively easy, as I had a solid group of runners with me and we were running with a great purpose. I relinquished my dowel rod only once (to a wonderfully charming 2:53 PR marathoner named Dana) as I made a pit stop, but soon caught up. As Dana handed me the dowel rod, she mentioned how nerve racking it had been for that quarter of a mile, and while I know she was joking I think she might have realized the responsibility I had on my shoulders. Often, I have heard of pacers who go out far too fast or exceedingly slow and I had vowed to never do that. In spite of the hills we encountered, I kept the group on a steady pace (in spite of some wind we encountered) and took us through the first half not one second off of a 3:10 pace.

In the next few miles my herd thinned out. I was rather disappointed. I knew that not all of these who tried were going to succeed but I nonetheless had visions of 30 of us crossing together, jockeying for overall position and all qualifying for Boston together. Part of the cause for this fall-off, was a not-so-flat-as-it-appeared-on-the-website second part of the course. The race director at the course briefing had warned us during the expo but it did not help us much here.

While some people also complained of a lack of spectators on a section through some parks, I found the wind that had picked up to be far more daunting. As each mile passed, I lost one runner and then another. Soon I was running alone.

I was still holding the sign, which had been blown all around by the wind, and my hand was extremely sore. I had not dropped the sign because every time we encountered a crowd, they cheered like mad and our pace picked up ever so slightly. However, even though I no longer had a single runner with me, when I noticed I was a smidgen off my 3:10 pace, I decided to pick it up. I soon caught one of the only few people I could see in front of me. Seth, as I learned his name later, turned to me and asked: "Are we on 3:10 pace?" I said, "A little off. But follow me and you are going to Boston."

Having said something similar to many people and having seen them disappear behind me, I was hoping Seth would be different. He did not let me down. Miles 23 and 24 were 6:51 and 6:50 respectively, almost completely erasing the time deficit. A misplaced marker at 24 elicited a worried look from Seth. But I told him to ignore his watch, ignore the markers and soon he would get a chance to run in the granddaddy of them all.

Mile 25 came upon us and almost immediately the wind picked up again. I could hear Seth straining. He was wearing headphones, so he probably was not aware that I could hear his labored breath. Due to construction, the course had been slightly modified and we had to do one of those dastardly things where you can see the finish line but have to run away from it before coming back to it. Just awful.

However when we rounded the corner and mile 26 passed us, I told Seth to go get it. I backed up a step so Seth could enjoy this moment by himself but it would not have mattered much: Seth took off on a sprint. I eased in a few seconds behind him in a 3:10:12, my second fastest time of Fiddy2. More importantly Seth now has to get plane tickets to Boston.

Dana found me minutes after the race .

"Thank you," she said.

"Why?" I asked.

She said, "I haven't sniffed a 3:10 in years, and following you in helped me finish in 3:11:30.

I told her that she has a PR that begins in "2", so it does not matter what she has been sniffing lately! While I did not get the photo finish of a horde of 3:10ers, I did get two victories under my belt for my pacing job. And yes, I held that damn dowel rod the whole way.

After the race, I walked half a block to my hotel (taken care of by the wonderfully generous people of the Des Moines Marathon, who treated me like a king the entire weekend), showered, and came back down to cheer some friends on.

I laughed when one of them said: "I ran a 3:40. How the hell are you showered and dressed already?"

38

Racing My Way to a Sub-3

Marathon 42

Race: Niagara Falls Marathon, Buffalo, NY to Niagara Falls, ON
Miles from home: 463.4
1,100.4 miles raced
262 miles to race

Finishing Time: 2:59:48
Place: 30th

It was wonderful to be recognized in print by Ripley's Believe it or Not when their publicist said: "We've had a lot of amazing athletes and people obsessed with breaking sports records, but we've never had anything like this".

One week before the race, the surrounding area got hit with 2 feet of snow. Talk about timing!

The logistical nightmare that could have been the Niagara Falls Marathon was averted mostly because of a running friend named Mike (mentioned in the Quad Cities recap) and various members of his family, to whom I am eternally grateful. From rides both to and from Niagara Falls to the Buffalo Airport to wonderful pizza provided after the race (and a warm shower as well), I just wanted to thank them personally here.

My accommodations were at the Great Wolf Lodge, made possible by good friends with connections. This expansive hotel/indoor waterpark/arcade/ baseball field/ blimp landing station was so new it still had smelled new. (Ok, I made the last two up but this place was enormous.)

Mike and I ventured into the casino to pick up our packets and quickly dispatched with the necessaries of getting our gear. Then it was time to play Blackjack. In twenty minutes I had made most of the money needed to buy a plane ticket to Dallas later in the year. Always knowing when to fold them in a casino, I quickly beat feet and considered myself fortunate to have this little bit of luck at the beginning of the weekend.

We grabbed a Niagara Falls Review. I had been told there would be an article about Fiddy2 in it. Thinking I might have to search the sports pages beneath curling and the local Bingo tourney to find the article, I was shocked to see not only a huge picture of me staring down the Leadville mountains, but see it taking up the entire top half of the page. Above the fold! I beat out hockey! In Canada!

Follow this up with a wonderfully written page in the handout given to all athletes participating in the various races of the weekend and I am completely convinced that Canada loves Dane. I may move north.

My goal for the weekend was semi-secret but most people knew I had been itching to break three hours. Of course, I never thought it was a possibility until the 3:05 I ran at Johnstown. I had eschewed the possibility of doing so the week prior in Des Moines and while I knew I might have a shot at it at the Marine Corps Marathon in a week, I knew getting it here would be deliciously sweet. I was put at ease talking to a marathon newbie on the bus ride to Buffalo and felt that perhaps today was the day (She ran her first marathon in a 4:56, so way to go Danielle!)

With this at-ease feeling, I toed the line. After a quick rendition of both the Canadian national anthem and the US anthem sung by the same wonderful woman, we were off. I told Mike I was going to give 6:52 minute miles a shot (exactly a 3 hour marathon), and took off. While I did not see much of Mike on the course, he was right behind me for quite some time.

178

The first four miles weaved us through some downtown sections of Buffalo right near the Art Gallery starting line. Evidence of the snowstorm that hit Buffalo a week before was everywhere. Downed trees and splintered limbs were brushed to the side of streets in snow piles, which still dotted the road in spite of the recent thaw.

Around mile five, we crossed the Peace Bridge into Canada and met the only real hill to speak of. A native French-speaking woman named Nathalie appeared by my side and in hesitant English asked me: "What is your projected finish time?" I told her I wanted to run a sub-3 and she said "Good. We help each other." Before the weekend, a good friend of mine who is French-speaking and a native Canadian, (from the exquisitely named town of Asbestos) had told me she would be with me in spirit. Now, I had her doppelganger running right next to me!

After running together a few miles I found that this Natalie had a 2:55 PR and had run just a few seconds shy of breaking 3 hours the last time she ran the Niagara Falls Marathon. I realized as we finished crossing the bridge that this woman was a better runner than I was and I had to make sure she did not take me out too fast. Sub-3 was all I wanted; it did not have to be 2:54!

Rounding off of the bridge and into a stiff headwind, Nathalie was smiling.

"Wind at our back on the way home," she said.

After the loop off of the bridge and a few miles of running south, the rest of the marathon was due north. And right now that appeared to be the way the wind was blowing. After weather predictions of awful wind and rain all weekend, this was a welcome thought indeed.

Nathalie and I ran the next few miles together but the quartet miles of 6:38, 6:39, 6:44 and 6:41 proved to be too fast for my tastes and I bid her adieu. (Ooh, look! I used French!) I had settled into a zone, which I did not want to break. I recently read a posting by one runner who said that calling a marathon at least 50% mental (something I have said often) is a crutch for the untrained. Well, all I know is that I set my mind to running 6:52s and the next thing I knew I had cruised through the first half with more than a minute to spare. This was not just the result of training but the fact that I told myself I wanted to run fast today. I felt I could do it and neither the cold temps, spotty rain or intermittent wind was stopping me. So far.

My friend Mauriella had made the 2- hour plus drive all the way up from Erie just to sit in one spot, in the rain, with a homemade sign to cheer me on as I passed. Her knowing smile that she had completely surprised me seemed to tell me that my shock was worth the trip.

While I hate "banking time" as I feel it is a bad running strategy, the fact remained that after mile 16 or so I had an extra 85 seconds in my safety deposit box. Doing some math in my head, I realized if I did not dip into my savings until the last 4 or 5 miles I could run 7:15s and still make the coveted time.

One of the great things about this race was the guaranteed water stops every mile in the second half of the race. While neither hungry nor thirsty, I would grab at least a swallow of liquid at these stops. I considered it my reward for running another 6:52 or less every mile.

Mile 18 was my first 6:53; one second over my pace. I was disappointed but rebounded with a 6:50 on the next mile and I think I actually smiled. Mile 20 loomed and with it the last 10k, where many a marathon hope has been dashed like ships between Scylla and Charybdis. Hitting this mile with a time of 2:16 and change (my fastest ever 20 miles in a marathon) I knew I was close to my goal. I had left myself with very little breathing room but it was indeed a possibility. Which of course means, the next two miles went by almost in slow motion as I ran a 7:10 and a 7:09. I almost screamed out loud in frustration at the massive loss of time in just those two miles.

My goal was slipping away. I cannot put into words how frustrated I would be if I just missed going under 3 hours. Actually, yes I could and it would look like Sarge yelling at Beetle Bailey: ("@*$#!")

People who had been leading me all day were coming into focus. I assumed that they were all gunning for 3 hours as well but they were not going to make it running at the pace they were. I would normally shout some words of encouragement and possibly try to drag them along with me. However so focused on my own race, I have to admit a bit of selfishness. I did not care who beat me or who lost to me as I just wanted that sub-3.

At mile 23, the thought of not being able to make it crept into my mind. My

180

math calculations showed me probably coming in at a 3:00:20. I am pretty sure I gave a disdainful glance heavenward, as if to say, "You let me come this far to fail?"

Giving everything I had without risking total collapse I headed into the last few miles. Yet in spite of this effort I was shocked when the next mile was only 7 minutes even, not even close to how fast it felt.

Two miles to go and I passed a few more runners. Mile 25 mercifully appeared in the distance and with 1.2 miles to go, I had 8:24 to traverse the distance. For those of us who hate math, that equates to exactly a 7 minute mile and exactly a 7 minute mile pace for that final .2. That last .2 sounds like nothing to the unknowing but forgetting to factor that distance into your total time means you will be extremely surprised and severely disappointed when you have to deal with that additional 90 seconds at the end. I caught sight of the plume of the falls off to my right, clenched my teeth and let go of all the energy I had left in my body.

I sprinted down the avenue next to the river feeding the falls and upon hitting the 13-mile marker (set up for the half marathoners), knew for the first time all day that sub-3 was mine. I shouted as I crossed the finish line in 2:59:48, more in relief than in exuberance.

The cheering crowd and the announcer who told them what I was doing this year were both lost on me, as I was wrapped in my own thoughts. While my main goal was obviously to raise money for L'Arche Mobile, I would have been lying if I said I did not want to run fast as well.

As I have said many times, there are many things you can not do in this world; trying is not one of them.

After giving a brief interview to Michigan Runner TV, I saw Nathalie. I shouted, "I DID IT!" and she gave me a big hug. But then she was whisked away to an interview of her own (because of her fourth place female finish). I myself had finished thirtieth overall but the only thing that mattered was the number that started in "2".

Dane shocks himself with a 6 minute personal best and runs his first sub-3 hour marathon ever...in his 42nd marathon of the year at the Niagara Falls Marathon.

39

Amongst
the Monuments

Marathon 43
Race: Marine Corps Marathon, Arlington, VA
Miles from home: Technically, 0.
1,126.6 miles raced
235.8 miles to race

Finishing Time: 3:03:54
Place: 167th

I was the fastest person named "Dane" in this race. While said usually as a joke, I did have to beat out 3 others this time.

Luckily my apartment is at mile 2 and not mile 20 of the course or I might have been just been tempted to go home. For the first time in nearly six months I slept in my own bed the night before the marathon. The day before the marathon, I sat on my couch and ate food from places I knew. The morning of the marathon I woke up and went to a race about 1.5 miles away. It was this trio of events and many like them that made me realize why many people who are impressed with what I was doing (or what others like Dean Karnazes are doing) are, in fact, impressed. Allow me to explain.

I am quite sure there are indeed more than a handful of people that could run a marathon every weekend with fairly good times. I have seen it illustrated that some of the great runners in the past averaged 26 plus miles a day for weeks on end in some of their hardest training periods. However, there is a reason why running a marathon race every weekend impresses many: because I am not doing it as a training run where I leave and return to my own apartment. I am traveling to whereever the race is, running it, coming home, going to work and then doing it all over again. It then dawned on me why those who are not impressed may not be. Chances are they are thinking: "Hey, I could get up every Saturday and run 26.2 miles with no problem." That is just it. That is not what I was doing. And if I was, my goodness it would have been so much easier. And I have not even begun to add in the fundraising and all that goes into successfully doing that.

You see this weekend I had no travel snafus. This weekend, I did not have to fly anywhere. I did not have to see if there was anywhere I could eat that would not upset my stomach. Instead, I went to Target. I bought some jeans and a paper shredder. I went out with friends for dinner. The racing aspect of the weekend was completely in the back of my mind (as much as it could be) and if not for one little snag I could have made this point even more eloquently. More on that to come.

I let it be known to anyone who listened that I wanted to break three hours again. In fact, I wanted to break it the rest of the year. I now knew that even in the tail end of my year a sub-3 was a very attainable goal. Of course, some people obviously feel a 3-hour marathon is jogging, but I still find it to be a little trying. Maybe if I took some time off from work or changed my goals whenever something did not work out my way, it would be easier.

However, regardless of any of this, the simple fact remains the Marine Corps Marathon is one of my favorite marathons. While neither a dove nor a hawk, there is something about our armed forces that I will forever defend and cherish.

The course is wonderful too in terms of sights to be seen but it is by no means a walk in the park (even though you pass through a few of them.) A rather tough hill hits you at mile two and you have a desolate, always-windy section on Hains Point and numerous other difficult points to traverse. However, in my short history of marathoning, I have found fewer races that can even come close to matching the sheer number, volume and intensity of the spectators who line this course. For this and many other reasons, I will return often to run the Marine Corps Marathon.

When a superb rendition of our National Anthem was belted out the 20 plus thousand people who were previously milling around suddenly stop jockeying for position and simply stood transfixed, I was moved beyond words. I was ready to run a great race.

The first few miles went exactly as planned. Fully hydrated, I made what I would hope would be my only pit stop around mile four and quickly rejoined the fray. Down through Arlington and past my apartment, I smiled as my good friends Anne and Elaine shouted out words of encouragement. A surprise hello came from my friend Sara as I made the turn down onto Spout Run Parkway, an almost completely downhill section that makes up for the uphill at mile two. Soon, we passed over the Key Bridge (my daily commute to work at the time) into historic Georgetown and onto the Rock Creek Parkway.

This is where we first saw some of the leaders. A few miles of an out and back section allowed just enough time for me to start up the "out" that they were heading "back" on. One of the wonderful things about the Marine Corps Marathon is the talent it attracts for absolutely no prize money. The winner only gets bragging rights.

Before I knew it, I was down into the six deep crowds surrounding the Lincoln Memorial and taking in all the splendor of D.C. Many changes had been made to the course over the past few years and a recent one was to assure the bigger hill around Capitol Hill was removed from the course. Many of us (I am guessing all, actually) appreciated it.

I hit the halfway point about a minute faster than last week but was keeping my excitement in check. We had already experienced a fair amount of wind on the course and I just knew Hains Point might be treacherous. Nevertheless, here and there I would extol the crowds to cheer for me and other runners and ride the wave of their cheers to the next gathering of spectators. Seeing Anne and Elaine again as they screamed in unison helped too.

Just as I figured, Hains Point provided a very flat, relatively unoccupied 3 or

4-mile stretch of nothingness. I understand why this section is so bereft of spectators (it is almost impossible to go there and still make it back to see your runner finish) but when people ask me where I need help most, there are two sections I always mention: the Hains Point area followed by the 14th Street Bridge and the mile around the Pentagon where you feel like you are isolated from everything.

Another thing I was correct about was the wind on Hains Point (for me anyway; I later found out the swirling wind died down or was at the back of runners later in the day). I am unsure of the speed of the gusts that hit me head-on; all I know is that it was tough.

I turned up the onramp and entered the dreaded 14th Street Bridge. Many hate this 1.5-mile stretch of undulating concrete and wind. Luckily for me I knew my good friend Christine was waiting for me with my beloved Propel. I needed a wind blocker more than I needed liquid. However, the Propel gave me a burst and I hit mile 22 a minute or so faster than I had a week prior. Wow. All I had to do was average a 7-minute mile the rest of the way and I would have yet another PR!

I looked at my watch when I hit the next mile marker. 7:30. Damn. Mile 23 more or less eroded any chance that I had of setting a PR. On a normal run, that loss of time would not be fatal. Today was different. The heavy wind on mile 23 became more fierce along the empty parking lot of the Pentagon. I climbed another onramp and two women passed me in quick succession. More wind stood me straight up. I actually laughed out loud at the absurd power of this gust and entered the last stretch of highway. Making matters worse, I knew I still had the challenge of that final steep hill leading to the Iwo Jima Memorial and the finish line. Some of my running club buddies cheered me on at this point but there would be no personal best today.

I crossed the finish in 3:03:54, my second fastest time ever. What I recall most from this entire race was how it was not even until mile 21 that I realized "Hey, it is mile 21!" Why? Because a lot of the usual pressure I face (making it back to the plane, hoping someday to break 3 hours, etc.) was alleviated. I was out hoping to run my best time and was only focused on that. But I took the 3:03 and went home. All 1.5 miles away.

"You have to have fun, or it is a long 26.2 miles," Dane says.

40

Running Around Lance

Marathon 44
Race: New York City Marathon, New York, NY
Miles from home: 231
1,152.8 miles raced
209.6 miles to race

Finishing Time: 3:05:43
Place: 1199th

My Race:

- The finishing temperature was 52 degrees.
- The Lottery on marathon Sunday in New York was worth 52 million.

Seeing a good friend who put me up (and not needing to shell out a grand for a hotel) was one of the highlights of the whole weekend in New York. Thank you so much, Heather.

I arrived early on Friday, made it to the expo and got a rubdown from Patrick Materna with The Stick, a product that has helped me greatly. You see, after the Marine Corps Marathon last weekend I, for the first time all year, did not run a single lick for a whole week. What had been building after the races in Colorado finally came to a head in general muscle fatigue. Terrel Hale, a massage therapist who has kneaded my muscles weekly and had been invaluable to me in the past few weeks, had his hands full (literally) with an enormous knot in my right calf and a strained shin muscle. For the first time all year, I had trepidation going into a marathon about whether it would be an injury-free finish. But as I walked around NYC on Saturday with Heather, everything felt pretty good. The legs were far from great but better than they had been earlier in the week.

Morning broke the day of the race (or night was barely over) and I readied myself for the marathon. One of the problems with races like New York and Boston are the logistics of actually getting to the race. While NYC is at 10 am, I still had to be up at 4 am in order to guarantee I would get to the start on time via the bus transportation.

Luckily, my friend Christine met me at the bus pick up at 6 am (she also provided me with transportation to and from DC, which was a godsend) for some much needed early morning conversation. We kept each other company for the next three hours as the buses went from Manhattan to Brooklyn, to God only knows where until we landed on Staten Island. Here Christine and I met her friend Nattu who had run 28 miles the day before and was using the marathon on Sunday as a training run for a 100 mile race he planned to compete in next weekend. We kept ourselves entertained until it was time for us to split into our respective corrals.

I was well aware NYC would be bigger than any other race I had ever done but I was not prepared for the sheer volume of people around me at all times. Of course, it did not help that in spite of the fact that we are supposed to be in our corrals by number (and therefore marathon time) I saw many people wearing bib numbers in the 13,000s who were in my 3,000-numbered corral. Few things anger me more than this.

With orange-bib wearers and blue-bib wearers going onto the top of the bridge for the start and we greenies hitting the lower half, we crammed together and waited for the gun. As the weather got a little warmer, runners started shedding their shirts and pushing towards the front. You could feel the anticipation in the air. It was electric.

The gun went off and to the strains of "New York, New York" I got to the start line in about 20 seconds. Unfortunately, as I mentioned before, there were hordes of people who were not where they were supposed to be. Subsequently, I was bobbing and weaving and running on the curbs just to get around Luis VanCheaterson and get into my groove.

The first few miles passed by rather quickly and here is where the surprises started. The runners simply did not thin out. Unlike last week at Marine Corps, where, within minutes I was running with just a few runners, in NYC I was always fighting for position. People were stepping on my feet, cutting me off and running elbow-to-elbow everywhere. This is something I have never experienced eight miles into a race.

Another thing I was not used to was Lance Armstrong. Please understand this: I am a Lance fan. I am not, however, a fan of the Lance Cam. You see, during the race, Lance had a dedicated cameraman and motorcycle leading the way through the crowd. If this had been at, say, the Marine Corps Marathon it would not have been a problem. Unfortunately, as I said, there were masses of people everywhere. Double unfortunately, Lance's plan was to run a sub-3. Why is that unfortunate? Because that was my plan too.

So when I passed him at mile 8 and settled down into a comfortable pace, not only was I jostling for position like everyone else, I had this damn LanceMobile right behind me. Every few seconds it would let out a little honk to clear the path if it got a little too congested or you got a little too close to the entourage. Another obviously irritated runner said a few not so kind words (which I agreed with) but laughed when I tried to lighten the mood by calling it our "Honking Pace Reminder."

I could have dropped back but that was not really an option for two reasons. First, this was the pace I wanted to run. You should never let anyone else dictate your pace. Second, running behind a police escort and breathing in its fumes for 138,336 feet was not something I was inclined to do. So, I decided to push it a little harder than I wanted to and move ahead of the caravan. Maybe I'd find an extra gear.

However, so did Lance. For the next 5 miles I had to deal with the Honking Pace Reminder (HPR). My final words on this are: I am happy Lance ran the

190

race. I am happy that many people probably used him as an unofficial pacer. (Hell, he did have some serious running celebrities with him. I stared more than once at Joan Benoit Samuelson and Alberto Salazar and secretly wished they would pace me!) However, everyone in a race deserves to run unimpeded and this caravan was not allowing that. That said, when Lance passed me right before the half I was hoping I would see him again near the end.

As we set foot onto the longest straightaway of the course (4 miles up 1st Avenue), I knew Heather (and her husband and dog) was waiting for me on 80th Street. Then further down my good friend Diana would be ready to cheer me on at 103rd. Good thing because the wall came early in New York. When Heather and her gang took some pictures and flashed a huge Fiddy2 sign, the posing I gave them masked how tired I was. I used the knowledge that 20 blocks away Diana would be waiting for another pick me up. Ironically I picked her out of the crowd long before she saw me (in spite of her frantically searching the runners) and I had to give her a little tug on her shirt as I ran by.

Another bridge (and therefore a hill; sometimes we forget that bridges can be the worst hills) took us into the Bronx. While not nearly as populated with spectators, the Bronxians (Bronxites?; Bronxodians?) were just as rambunctious. Sample:

Bronx Chick (serious Bronx accent): "You go, Fiddy2."
Me: "Know-what-I'm-sayin'?"
Bronx Chick: "Mmhmm. That's right!"

Just around mile 21 a pair of ridiculously sculpted calf muscles passed me. Sure enough, it was my friend Dean Karnazes. In case you don't know, Dean was completing his fiftieth marathon distance in fifty days, ending in NYC on Sunday. Our exchange:

Me: "Karno!"
Dean: "What's up brother? I expected you to be up there beating Lance."
Me: "Yeah, me too. Not my day. You look great, though. Don't let me stop you."
Dean: "See you at the finish." And then he was gone. And I mean gone. Dean ran what had to be a sub 42-minute final 10k. While I tried keeping with him (he may be a friend but I still wanted to beat him) Dean was too strong for me and my legs were too tired. In spite of rapidly depleting energy stores it was

the pain in my muscles that had me worried. Throughout the year, whenever I felt something might be a problem muscle-wise, I have forced myself too remember I have "X" amount of marathons left in the year. In this case it was eight more. So Dean disappeared and so did my shot at running my second fastest marathon ever.

Still mindful of my leg problems, I had an outside shot at a 3:04 (a number I have never ran in a marathon) so I thought I would give it a try. I picked up the pace. Then we entered Central Park.

Was it the hills that slowed me down? Nope, it was the crowds. Why, you ask? Because I began having an absolute ball! Flexing for the crowd, running over to high five spectators, throwing my hands in the air to extol them to cheer, I wanted to thoroughly enjoy the huge gathering of people and at the same time let them know they were appreciated. I even saw a Fiddy2 sign being held by no one I knew. While feeling good, I did not feel good enough to stop and ask them who they were (like I did in Mississauga). I regret not doing so. (My legs do not.)

Down a hill, up another hill, turning out of the park and then finally back into it, I was enjoying the heck out of this race. Waving to the crowd like I was someone who mattered (and they cheered like I was because I am apparently convincing), I pulled into a 3:05:43, good enough for the fourth fastest time of my life. I learned Dean had flown to a 3:00:30 (just an incredible burst of speed) and Lance got his sub-3 but later proclaimed it was the hardest physical endeavor he has ever done.

This is the cancer-surviving, seven-time Tour De France winner. Makes you feel good about finishing your forty-fourth marathon of the year just a few minutes behind him.

41

Five Years of Marathons

Marathon 45
Race: Richmond Marathon, Richmond, VA
Miles from home: 104.9
1,179 miles raced
183.4 miles to race

Finishing Time: 3:12:38
Place: 78th

Five years ago (to the day), I ran my first marathon. Five years ago (to the day), my grandmother passed away. Thirty-two years ago (almost to the day), my father was crippled in a hunting accident. You can see that November 11th holds significance in my life. I am aware that dates and anniversaries help us put things in perspective but they mean less to me than they do to others. Still, It is hard to ignore major occurrences in one's life like the ones listed above. And it is ironic that very specific lessons I learned five years ago would come into play on this very same race day.

I could tell even before the race started that I was in for a tough day For the second straight week, I took the entire week off from running in an effort to heal my aching legs. A busier than normal workweek did not help any, nor did the one less day of rest. (Richmond was run on a Saturday.)

On Friday I left work, and began to head to Richmond on the 85mph moving parking lot that is 95 South. I stayed with my friend Greta and her boyfriend Matt, and had a chance to see my running friend Katie. Quite the runner herself, we devoured some homemade pasta and all hit the sack.

Right before the race I could not locate a sign I was going to wear honoring both of my passed grandparents. I then realized I had also forgotten my sunglasses. An inauspicious beginning to say the least.

A few runners said they were very much in awe of Fiddy2. Not only the running, they said, but the coordination and the money I had raised so far. I was pleased to meet them all and wished them the best of luck.

With the race underway, my fears of the projected warm temperatures soon became reality. I realized there was nothing to do but drink lots of liquids and hope. As mile two lead to mile file and then to mile 10, I have never been so tired so early in a race. I kept waiting for the haze in my mind to blow away and for the energy to arrive.

I am not quite sure why they call it a flat course. While not mountainous, there are plenty of rolling hills. I do not think I can accurately rate the course itself, given the temperature of the day. There were spots that were just lovely and I am sure I would have thoroughly enjoyed them more if I had not been so miserable so early. The volunteers and spectators for a relatively small marathon were just great. Knowledgeable volunteers and lively crowds really were a treat

I knew my friend Christine was waiting for me at the halfway point and that kept me going. With a Propel in hand, I saw her snap a few quick pictures before handing me my elixir. Coming to a dead stop, I told her how weary I was and she replied that I was drenched in sweat. There was nothing to do but down my drink, eat an energy gel, shrug my shoulders and move on. I was close to a sub 3-pace at this point but I knew that was a mirage.

At mile 16, after crossing a bridge not unlike the 14th Street Bridge in the MCM, Greta was waiting for me with her coffee-in-hand. With the course running less than 2 blocks from her house, she went back home after dropping

Katie and me off and settled in for the day. Her efforts were greatly appreciated and feeling better here than I had for miloo I gave her a big smile.

At mile, 18 Christine saw me for the final time before the finish. Some guys in a nearby cafe gave a huge cheer for Fiddy2 and I flexed to show my appreciation. I found out later that Christine had told them what I was doing and their cheer was a result of her efforts. However, even this cheer did little to stave off my exhaustion. The sun was beating down relentlessly from a cloudless sky and I was feeling it.

As the 3:10 pace group passed me one of them looked at my name written on my arm (courtesy of Christine) and shouted encouragement.

"Good job, Dane!"

Then they paused and one said, "Wait – Dane! You were in the newspaper!! Go DANE!"

I gave a smile.

With most of my goals out the window, I had one remaining: to run exactly one hour faster than I did in my first marathon five years prior. Looking at my watch, I knew it was going to be close. While the course finished on a downhill, this was only after a series of twists and turns in the city itself where the unknown was just around the bend. When I hit the finishing street I turned on the last of the low burning jets I had in reserve. Right then my friend Katharine surprised me by yelling out my name. She had made the trip down from DC just to cheer me on. I have some great friends.

Running the last .2 of a mile in 1:19 I cruised in, arms pointing at the sky in a 3:12:38. I have no doubt in my mind that my grandparents helped carry me that last 385 yards. In fact, I was so happy to get this last goal that I did not even hear the announcer talk about Fiddy2 over the loudspeaker.

The rest of the field wobbled in intermittently. Temperatures reached into the 80s. I was worried about Katie. However, she soon appeared and though a few minutes slower than she wanted to be, I think she was quite pleased given the heat.

After the race I spoke with a few other people who were just really impressed with Fiddy2. That took some of the sting off a "bad" day. I think my grandparents were impressed.

42

Gonna Fly Now

Marathon 46
Race: Philadelphia Marathon, Philadelphia, PA
Miles from home: 142.2
1,205.2 miles raced
157.2 miles to race

Finishing Time: 3:11:13
Place: 130th

Fifteen of my close friends live in Philly and I saw almost none of them. Yet, I randomly saw a law school acquaintance whom I hadn't seen in four years. I have apparently achieved "OH, you're that guy" status.

I could have driven to Philly Friday night to spend more time with a college and law school friend but the new James Bond movie opened Friday night and well, I do not miss opening nights of James Bond. Even if that means I have to go to the 10:05 show because it was sold out earlier. But Heather (my host for the weekend) is a big James Bond fan herself, and was not offended.

Very pleased with the movie, I headed up to Philly early in the morning to a nice deal on some new sunglasses at the expo, grabbed my bag and tried to relax the rest of the day. A nail biter for Penn State did not help at all, and while I rooted for a meteorite to hit the Horseshoe in Columbus so I would not have to actually root for either Ohio State or Michigan, alas nothing fell from the sky.

Hoping that the projected perfect weather, the extra day of rest from last week and intense massages from my man Terrel (who ran the JFK 50—miler himself the day before this race) would erase some of the pain in my legs and just flat-out feeling of weariness, I called it a semi-early night.

As promised, the weather was perfect for a race. A much larger crowd of runners than I expected was on hand and were chomping at the bit. "Just Two More Minutes to the start of the Philadelphia Marathon!" was shouted on three separate occasions, all more than two minutes apart. At least we think that was what was uttered. The PA System sounded like it was the lovechild of a Cold War Ukrainian Sub that had sunk, been brought to the surface, shipped to the States, stored in an warehouse like the Ark of the Covenant in Indiana Jones for six decades, dusted off Sunday morning and given a quick spit shine before use and well, something else that sounds really bad and noisy and useless (John Madden, perhaps). Honestly, those are the best speakers we can get, Philly?

No gun start signified anything as we were alerted to the race's commencement by the mass suddenly pushing forward. The runner in front of me, Oldy McWrongCorral, refused to budge for about the first 5 seconds, so I started off the marathon running longer than I needed to by going around him!

Either I consecutively ran one of the slowest third miles and fastest fourth miles of any marathon I have ever run, or the markers were a little askew. I haven't run a 5:19 ever in a marathon.

Crowds lined the streets of inner city Philly and were very enthusiastic as we marched down some street and turned onto another. I was less concerned with street names and more concerned with the fact that, while running some pretty decent splits, I did not have a snap in my step. I had not had the snap for quite some time.

If you think about every marathon I had run this year as half a mile, I was presently on mile 23 of the Fiddy2 "marathon"! But I was able to punch out my first sub-3 ever just a few weeks ago and if I was going to break down and run bad times I would think it would have happened sooner. So all kindo of body assessment was going on in the first few miles as I hoped the lethargy would lift.

While I missed her at mile five, Heather says she was there. She is, like, five feet tall so I will take her word for it.

A nice woman I had met in Charlottesville Marathon came up behind me around mile nine and asked me what I was hoping to run. I told her my hopeful time but then lay the mattress by stating I was already feeling tired and was pretty sure it was not going to happen. I told her to take off and wished her well. While she did not get the sub-3 she was hoping for, her 3:03:55 on a course that is not nearly as flat as advertised, was superb indeed.

At mile 16, I heard a familiar voice on the course. While at this point my mile splits were slipping and I had more or less conceded to not running a sub-3, it was a huge boost to see my college roommate Keith and his daughter on the sideline cheering me on. I thought about a hug and ran over to him for a second but I still had the competitive spirit in me spurring me on. So I settled for a quick high five. Now, if Keith had possessed a camera, I would have stopped just to get a picture of him wearing the gift I gave him in college, a blue t-shirt with white lettering that said: "Dane's My Roommate."

The thoughts of a sub-3 disappeared soon after as, in spite of the long slow downhill we were running, I could not take advantage of the downhills I love so much. The super nice rear end of some woman dressed all in hunter orange, who I had been using as motivation for close to half the race, slowly but surely pulled away from me and was replaced with the hairy back of some guy who might have been George "The Animal" Steele. (Guys aged 30-40 just laughed. Women have no idea who the heck I am talking about.)

I also saw another runner friend from online for the first time as he went blazing back from the turn around in Manayunk. We too exchanged high fives and he soared away in the opposite direction.

After the 20-mile turn around I knew that not only was a sub-3 dead but a 3:10 was going to be hard to get as well. The crowd was really supportive and ample through this little trendy section of Philly. Then I heard Eye of the Tiger blasting on a radio. There really are few songs better suited to pumping a person up. There is no doubt my faster mile split at this point was due in part to the sultry tones of Survivor.

Unfortunately, soon after this people began to pass me by the dozens. I simply did not have the juice. My legs felt like I was running in sand. I had all but decided that it was time to mail this one in. Something I always forget in races when I decide to dial it down is that I am not immediately going to feel great by doing so. Only stopping is going to feel "great."

Nevertheless, I would run fast on the surges of energy that surfaced here and there and tried to keep my mind off my pain. As this out and back section of the course allowed us to see many of the runners four, five and six miles behind us, I began shouting and cheering for everyone else. A few high fives here and there made me feel better even if it did nothing for the other runners.

I saw my gorgeous friend Lisa pumping out yet another marathon, a few people shouted out "Go Fiddy2!" and some older chap dressed in a tux from about 1947 went chugging by in the opposite direction.

A little trip along the Boathouse Row prepped me for the final surge.

A surge of energy made me decide to go for 3:10 anyway even though I knew the final hill made it all but impossible. As I began passing dozens of people I heard one girl yell to a guy in front of me: "Go!! I do not care what it takes but get that 3:10!" I passed him and the next thing I know he was at my side. I glanced sideways after looking at my watch and he let out, between breaths, "We going to get it?"

I sort of laughed while looking at the hill and said: "Nope. But let's fail spectacularly together." I have no storybook ending. But in finishing in 3:11:13 with him right at my heels, I was able to do a little detective work using his bib number and found out that he had indeed broken 3:10 with his chip time. I'll take credit for that.

43

A Run Through
the Woods

Marathon 47
Race: Northern Central Trail Marathon, Sparks Glencoe, MD
Miles from home: 71.3
1,231.4 miles raced
131 miles to race

Finishing Time: 3:09:54
Place: 18th

November, with only four marathons and very little running in between, comprised the least amount of mileage run by me for any month of 2006. With this marathon I conquered 11 months. Many, including myself, never thought I would be running Boston Qualifying times at this point.

I am convinced Maryland has the strangest names for its towns of any state or province out there. Sure, Canada has Medicine Hat and Moose Jaw, but those are just quirky and funny. But Lutherville Timonium? Cheverly? Boring? Crappo? These are really names of cities? Would you date a person who hailed from Crappo? And the start of this race: Sparks Glencoe. They may call it "Sparks" on the website but the post office says "Sparks Glencoe".

For the second straight week, the weather was perfect. A little frost was on the window of my car the morning of the race but the sun quickly melted that off. I met my friend Kira in the gym where we were picking up our timing "chips" before the start of the race (these were actually those prison house arrest anklets of which I am none too fond.) Kira had signed up for the race the day before hoping to bolster her resume to apply for the Badwater 135 mile race in Death Valley in July. And you thought I was crazy.

Also in attendance was my friend Cowboy Jeff sporting his Fiddy2 shirt. Jeff made the trip to the race and showed me tremendous support throughout by handing out flyers and getting rousing cheers from many of the spectators! Great guy. He had not mentioned he was going to be at the race but his hat gave him away immediately. In fact, he looks naked without and whenever he takes it off it is like he is missing a part of his head.

Speaking of costumes, I almost missed my friend the Pink Fairy. You see, he was running the race in ...gasp... shorts and a shirt!! No pink tutu, pink shoes or pink wand. Keith (which he says is his real name) was running his twenty-fifth marathon of the year!

Rachel, one of the race directors of the Frederick Marathon, tracked me down to say hello. A few people whom I had never had the chance to meet in person but had talked to endlessly online, introduced themselves. When we exited the Sparks Elementary School for the start I was wishing we had more time to talk.

Knowing that the course was supposed to be flat and fast (and also knowing race directors lie more than fisherman) I was curious what my legs would do on a short week of rest. Hoping to run another PR, I thought I would take it easy and hope that the "flat" section of the race coming back (i.e. mostly downhill) would allow me to negative split my time from the "flat" section of the first half (i.e., mostly uphill).

The race started and after a very fast first mile and change we ventured onto the mostly crushed gravel surface on which we would run 95% of the race. As much as others love trail and gravel, I prefer concrete and asphalt.

Mile after mile took us through wooded areas with a creek or river on one side and wildlife and trees on the other. My opinions on "scenic" courses are well known but given I did not expect too much from the day, I decided to look around a bit. While I never ran cross-country in high school this course looked like what it must have been like. Squirrels played tag, birds sang and I am pretty darn sure I saw a deer flit quickly across the trail up ahead. As the sunlight filtered in through the trees and warmed my body, I was having a very good time.

A few runners who had passed me earlier were coming into focus. To my legs and mind, the miles felt relatively fast but my watch told me otherwise. I was routinely running just over 7 minute miles when I felt I was running much faster. But I felt internally good. Perhaps I could indeed run a negative split after all.

In case you are curious, this was not a race to run if you need spectators. However, those volunteers who were at the aid stations were very helpful ("Gatorade on your right, water on your left!"), friendly and rather plentiful for being out in the middle of nowhere just 48 hours after Thanksgiving. A large helping of kudos goes out to the volunteers of the race.

A runner who I had passed earlier in the race came up on me around mile 15. Rich was this chap's name and he told me he was actually a cyclist. I told him that I was actually a swimmer and asked what the hell both of us were doing out here running.

As mile 17 approached I commented to Rick how good I felt. A sub 3:05 seemed to be well within grasp. The question was what would my time be. Like before on the front half of the course, my efforts put into each mile were not showing on the watch. I still felt great and expected to turn it on at the end.

I picked up the pace a smidgen to try and push through a faster time but I was all of a sudden spent! So I stopped, ate the Gu provided by the race in our packet, downed a full glass of water and then Gatorade.

A few yards down the path my good friend Danielle had tracked me and brought me a Propel. Having gone for a five mile run herself, she was look-ing all sporty in her running gear. I am sure she could have pumped out a few fast miles with me if she had not hopped back in the car to catch me at the finish.

In full catch-up mode, I passed four or five people as I began tracking down runners and make them pay for having gone out too fast. Few things feel better than just blasting by someone.

A completely unexpected fan and supporter almost made me lose my composure, as she was not supposed to have been able to make it to the race. Without a doubt, her presence helped push me through what was coming up.

You are kidding me right? We have to end on these hills? They did not seem this bad on the way out!

With one more guy in my sights who kept taking walk breaks I was startled to have someone pass me at a fast pace. Fully expecting him to be a relay person (they had been passing me throughout the day but most were kind enough to wear the RELAY tag on the back of their shirts), I was quite shocked to see he was not.

Time was slipping away and I knew the goals needed to be readjusted. I lost over a minute per mile as I slogged up these huge hills in the last two miles. Nothing like having a 3:06 in your grasp and watch it slip away.

To the friend who stopped by to cheer me on, I told her no matter what happened, I would run a Boston Qualifying time for her. I crossed the finish line in 3:09:56 and felt partially vindicated for having missed other goals. A second place in my age group also helped me lick my wounds.

I only had one month left.

44

Early Morning Heat

Marathon 48
Race: Cayman Islands Marathon, Grand Cayman Island
Miles from home: 1370
1,257.6 miles raced
104.8 miles to race

Finishing Time: 3:24:35
Place: 5th

In what could be called my first vacation or break of 2006, I picked a wonderful place to go if you love heat, sun and beaches. And I do, very much. Of course, many of my friends said they were jealous I was running a marathon in the Cayman Islands. However, these many friends were not marathoners (or were not thinking when they said it) or they would know that no one would be jealous of me running a marathon where it is hot and humid.

I arrived early in the Caymans to take some much-needed downtime. I did not want to waste too much energy before the race, for reasons both obvious and not but I knew I could not pass up an opportunity to enjoy this tropical paradise. My original travel companion for the trip couldn't make it. Another friend and multiple marathon supporter, Christine, was itching for some fun and sun. Shirking all of her real life duties she flew to meet me in the Caymans.

Good friend Mike McPheters and his family made the trip to this race as well. After realizing we were on the same connecting flight from Florida, I met up with Mike and wife Judy and their wonderful 4-year old daughter, Victoria. Looking over the race registrants we noticed we had a good shot at doing very well in the race. But there are always unknowns and late registrants so we kept our hopes low. Well, tried to anyway.

The wonderful race directors set up interviews for me and I pushed L'Arche Mobile's connection to Fiddy2 as much as possible even when the questions continued to revolve around how crazy I was, etc. People still tended to be more interested in my times and how many shoes I had gone through than why I had chosen L'Arche or why it means so much to me. Understandable. The former is a curiosity question while the latter requires a longer answer where I might ask them for a donation.

After an interview or two, Christine and I met with Mike and his family, as well as his brother John (a med student in Grand Cayman), for dinner at an all-you-can eat buffet where you only pay for your drink. Leave it to grad students to find such a wonderful place!

I enjoyed a low-key day before the race, soaking in some sun and trying to wind down for an early bedtime. With the 5 am start, I knew I had to be in bed by 8 pm. An absolutely great pasta dinner, which was included in the race fee, helped send me off to sleep, and dream of a win.

I had been hoping that the warm temperatures would drop by race day. But upon waking at 3:45 am I could see that it was not going to be the case. In fact, it was the warmest morning yet.

At the start line a sizeable crowd gathered consisting of racers, (the marathon field was nearly four times larger than the previous year, with a relay and half-marathon thrown in to boot, swelling the total number of competitors to over 300) countless volunteers and a surprising number of spectators. Pretty darn impressive crowd for a time I like to call Oh Dark Thirty.

Soon the race clock counted down to zero, and with a hearty cheer we plunged into the dark void of downtown George Town.

The RDs had strategically placed generator lamps to light the way on the course where there were no streetlights. As the first few miles clicked away in the darkness (it always feels like you are running faster when there is no light) it looked as if the race was going to play out the way I had hoped. You see, the previous year's runner-up, another runner, and I struck out stride for stride. Mike was right behind me, as was his brother John who was running the first leg of the relay for his team.

As we approached the first turn-around (the course was a 13.1 mile loop run twice), first and second place were right in front of me. I felt good. I knew a sub-3 was pretty much impossible. We were already teetering on being over that pace and there were 18 miles to go! However, with an approach of just beating whoever was out there, I was doing a good job of feeling out the competition and letting them set the pace.

As I made the turn around, I saw a male and female approaching me from the other direction. They looked totally in tune with each other and I assumed they would be competition for me soon. Little did I know that in about two miles they would pass me in unison. We exchanged pleasantries but I was a little crestfallen. The two others in front of me had already opened a sizeable lead. I knew that the course could get rough ahead (because of the rising sun, not the course itself, which was extremely flat) but hoped to keep them in sight as long as I could.

As we neared the halfway point I could hear the footsteps of the lucky ones who were finishing the half marathon. Also, right before the half, another marathoner, Julia (a sweet lady who I talked to after the race) caught up to and passed me as well. While my leg had been aching most the race, it was the rapidly rising sun and the humidity that were wearing me down. I seriously envy those who do not get affected by running in these swamp-like conditions, as it plain and simply drains me. In spite of this, I still felt like I might make a run at the leaders later in the race.

I passed through the arch of balloons marking the halfway point as an announcer shouted everyone's name and hometown. Onlookers cheered loudly for everyone and away went lap number two.

I would be remiss if I did not mention Christine and her wonderful support throughout this race. Because the course was not closed to traffic (there was barely any at that time in the morning anyway) Christine was able to drive the course with me and provide any support I needed.

I kept Linda in my sights for the next few miles. At every aid station, she would slow to a walk to grab liquid. I would make up many yards as I grabbed my liquid and kept going. Of course, stopping at the aid stations would have been perfectly acceptable. A contest was sponsored by the race to give awards to the best Aid Station on the course. With titles like "The Mexicans" (people were dressed in true Mexican garb, shouted lots of "oles" and did that crazy "Aiaiaiaiaiaia" thing) to Dr. McDreamy and the Nurse McHotties at "Cay's Anatomy" (where the fully ahem staffed nurses' plunging necklines did an excellent job of distracting me) there was ample support from these wonderful aid stations.

To top it off, the refreshments given to runners were not only ice-cold (something I am sure the racers later in the day appreciated even more than I did) but they were doled out in full bottles, rather than small cups. As Gatorade and water were handed out in abundance, there was absolutely no reason you could not be properly hydrated on this course. I was impressed at how this detail was attended to in a race in only its fifth year.

However, even with all of this aid, it was seeing Christine driving along in the Audi every mile that was so refreshing. Having a handmade sign hanging out of the trunk of the car, Christine would rush ahead to aid stations and get all of them to cheer for me. Of course they would either say " Go Dean!!" or "Way to go Dave!" It made me smile nonetheless. Even more important was the towel she had the foresight to bring that she would hand to me to wipe off both the water I had dumped over my head as well as my sweat.

And sweat I did. At mile 7, Christine mentioned I was leaving a trail of wet footprints behind me on a completely dry road!

But the largest help Christine gave was as a spotter. She told me that the guy who had been in first place was in serious trouble. This meant little to me as my own energy was waning. But when she added: "It is mile 15 and anything can happen." I put my head down and took off.

Soon enough, just as Christine said, the guy appeared in the distance. Before much more time passed both Julia and I sped by him. Christine had also told me that she thought that only the lead woman and the lead man were in front of me. This confused me to some extent as she described the lead man NOT as the guy who had been churning along with the female previously.

 As we approached the turn-around, the mystery was solved. The lead man and woman were in fact not the couple that had been running together the last time I saw them. Instead it was last year's runner-up and the lead woman that were now running stride for stride. The other chap had fallen back, looking tired and vulnerable. As Julia and I made the turn, I stopped for a tall cool bottle of Gatorade for the final push and asked if it was too late to sign up for the relay.

It is amazing what hindsight does for you. I am pretty sure that stopping for that Gatorade was the worst thing I could have done. For whatever reason, my legs tightened and I seemed to lose a ton of energy. Moreover, Julia started to pull away and other competitors quickly made up ground. This combination of factors hit me like a ton of bricks, as did the sun. (I made a suggestion to the Race Staff that since we are getting up at for a 5 AM race time anyway, why not push it back to 4:30 AM. Thirty fewer minutes in the sun.)

All I could think about was holding onto third place as my legs began to feel like lead. I once again hit that place in the marathon where I wonder why I put myself through this. Christine told me I had a two-minute lead on the next guy behind me but I knew it would not last. Soon, looking like a sad puppy who did something wrong, she informed me that he was now 50 meters behind me. While she told me later that she really felt awful breaking that news to me, I knew it was inevitable. Sure enough, at mile 22, he passed me.

Around mile 23, I just started walking. It was a gorgeous day in spite of my waning energy. I grabbed the towel from Christine and my beloved Propel and sauntered along. The guy in front of me started to disappear. I have to admit I gave up at this point. The combination of walking while drinking made for a very slow next mile. Almost 10 minutes to be exact. I told Christine there was no way I could catch the guy but she said again, "You never know. Go get him. You look great!" She is an excellent liar.

However, after taking off (a term I use lightly as it was more like leaning down on my legs and using them to push me forward in slow motion) I felt a little bit better. As I turned a corner, lo and behold, the guy in front of me was walking. Slowly! But I had less than a mile and half to make up what seemed like an insurmountable distance. To make matters worse, sensing danger, he looked back, saw me charging and started running again. Damn you, I thought.

In a move that would keep her from actually seeing the finish but undoubtedly helped provide me with a surge, Christine stopped about mile 25, asked if I needed anything more and told me to go get him.

As we turned into the downtown area with twists and turns almost every block it was hard to tell if I was gaining on him. Around a traffic circle, next to an empty parking lot, dodging a truck filled with re-bar which was going to parallel-park in front of me regardless of whether it hit me or not, I charged on. The balloon arch appeared just ahead. The runner was just in front of me.

The rest is a blur except for the finish times:

5. Rauschenberg, Dane Arlington, VA 3:24:35
6. McGeough, Paul, Grand Cayman 3:24:36

Hardly the victory I envisioned in the days before the race but an effort I am proud of nonetheless. This was my first race over 3:20 since August, when I was racing at high elevation, but I was happy.

Usually my experience ends here as I am on my way to the airport. However, I witnessed every racer coming in and what a treat it was. Over the loudspeaker the announcer stated each runner's name and a huge roar would erupt from the crowd. Every single time. All the way to the last two finishers, at just over 6 hours, the crowd's enthusiasm never waned. It was an awe-inspiring experience and I am sure every runner was happy to be a part of it.

As the Cayman press made a wonderful deal out of me running this race, I posed for pictures left and right. I told them they needed to get better stars to the island if I was that big a draw!

45

Running Royalty

Marathon 49
Race: Dallas White Rock Marathon, Dallas, Texas
Miles from home: 1326
1,283.8 miles raced
78.6 miles to race

Finishing Time: 3:09:36
Place: 121st

While I had been rather inefficient in knocking off new states during Fiddy2, this was my first in Texas.

Without a doubt, dipping under that 3-hour barrier in Niagara Falls was both a release and a curse. No longer was I left wondering if I could run that fast during the course of 52 marathons in one year. I could acquiesce to a slower time one week thinking I have many more left to give another sub-3 a shot. But here I was before this race with only four more marathons to go to again accomplish the feat. Thinking about how few marathons I had left would sometimes baffle me. I could barely recall a time when Fiddy2 was not my life.

Time on my hands during runs often led to questions. Could I have run much faster without working 50 plus hours a week? Does spending most of my evenings recapping, promoting and searching for sponsors for Fiddy2 sap my energy? Am I realizing that I really did sacrifice an entire year of my life? Yes and Yes and Yes. But I was so glad I had done so. I was both mentally and physically exhausted but I still hoped every week to break 3 hours again. Moreover, I had advanced so far in the year that I was now surprised when I did not do so. I call it marathon-amnesia. It is the state of mind that, even if the course or weather makes a race difficult a runner will say, "Yeah, but I still should have run faster."

So once again I had to wake up at a god-awful hour to board a flight. I was beat. The course did not look forgiving. I had lingering leg problems. But I had every intention of going out the next day and pushing the first half well under 90 minutes and still expecting to get faster in the second half. Why? Because every problem and excuse I listed means nothing to me once I toe the line. You see I have a race to run.

What a pasta dinner! The spread put on by the marathon felt like a four star banquet with multiple choices of pasta, excellent salad, dim lighting and a ballroom atmosphere. This is to say nothing about the various running dignitaries on both the dais at the front of the hall, as well as those available to rub shoulders with afterwards.

Dick Beardsley gave a rousing speech about the beneficiary of the Dallas White Rock Marathon, the Scottish Hospital. He described the many "handicapped" people he encountered at this hospital that he described as anything but.

A vision-impaired gentleman was profiled who had run this race many times at the speed many of us with full vision wish we could.

The local news interviewed many of the runners in the race and a broadcast of the show was beamed into the ballroom. Interviewing these runners and talking about the race itself was none other than Frank Shorter. Realizing this was not a live feed (given Shorter was seated on the dais amongst other runners) I almost tripped over a sprite of a female at the buffet line. Holy crap it was Joan Benoit Samuelson. My goodness!

For those of you who love movie stars this would be like meeting Brad Pitt.

For those who follow physics It would be like dinner with Stephen Hawking. Needless to say, while I am rarely a person to be star-struck, to even be in the room with these luminaries, let alone next to them in the chow line was humbling and enlightening. I introduced myself to "Joanie", as she is affectionately called by those who know her well (and some who don't) and told her that she was an inspiration to me. She asked me if I was running the marathon the next day and when I said I was and it was actually my forty-ninth of the year, she actually stopped putting pasta on her plate and took a second to look at me. That slight pause made me weak.

I knew I needed to speak to a few more of the racing legends. I could not pass up an opportunity like this. So, first up was Bill Rodgers (aka Boston Billy for his multiple successes at the Boston Marathon). I actually had no idea what I would say when I approached him, but he was soft-spoken and unassuming. Having brought nothing for him to sign, I remembered the Fiddy2 cards in my pocket and handed him one. To his credit, before signing the card, Bill actually looked it over and said, "Is this you?" When I told him it was he actually raised his eyebrows a pinch. I impressed (however slightly) Bill Rodgers!

We spoke about the intricacies of Fiddy2 and I recalled his quote: "No one with a full-time job will ever beat me in a race." I am sure he has heard his own words a multitude of times but I thought it was pertinent given the depth of our conversation. We spoke about how hard it is to run fast and work a regular job, let alone adding a fundraising aspect to the mix. What a pleasure that conversation was.

I next moved down the table to Dick Beardsley. Deeply involved in a conversation with another runner, I could see why he was chosen to be a speaker. His enthusiasm is immense, his desire to listen genuine, and his demeanor warm and inviting. We spoke about Fiddy2 as well and some other ultras I had done in the past few years. When he heard my times in those races, he said, "You have some talent! You need to get what you are doing out in the public." I told him that if a running legend like him is relatively unknown outside of running, that I had no chance. Regardless, for a man who has run a 2:08 marathon, he stilled seemed genuinely impressed with my endeavor. I was now beaming. While I wanted to talk forever, I felt I had occupied his time enough and excused myself to leave.

It was then that I noticed Frank Shorter sitting with a few people and chatting.

I was not able to get the entire conversation but he was saying something rather elegant in regards to steroid testing. Only wishing to get his autograph, I was quite surprised that when he asked for my name, the reporters sitting around him immediately ushered me to join them at this round-table discussion. Before too long, the reporters having heard of Fiddy2, they were asking me more in-depth questions about it. I felt a little awkward speaking about it given the company on hand. Nevertheless, Frank asked me a few questions himself before I, again not wanting to take too much time, excused myself from the table.

Finally, as I left the banquet hall I saw Jeff Galloway. In case you do not know, along with being an Olympian, Galloway revolutionized the training for many marathoners, enabling those not blessed with great talent to complete a marathon with a run/walk method. Say what you will about the plethora of runners running marathons these days or the soaring average marathon time but I know that he single-handedly is responsible for fewer obese people in this country. I told him this and again got another signed Fiddy2 card.

I walked away from these encounters on cloud nine. I had thoughts of really crushing this course. Too bad the drunken couple in the room next to me kept me up on and off all night until I finally had to take care of the situation. A few hours of sleep later I woke and readied for the race.

Given the elite bib number of 49 (for the 49th marathon I was doing this year) I was hoping I could earn it by running at least 49th overall. I was aware this was going to be difficult given the strength of the field (the course record was broken for both men and women with an overall winning time of 2:12.) As I settled into the crowd, near the front as one of the few white people, I saw Dick Beardsley standing next to me. We exchanged pleasantries and I asked him what he hoped to run. With a shrug he said: "in the 2:40s". I laughed and then told him I was going to sprint at the beginning so I could tell my friends I had led Dick Beardsley in a marathon. The gun went off and for 100 meters I did just that. Then I never saw him again (he ended up running a 2:49:41 to win the Masters Division. What a nice guy with incredible talent.)

Throughout the first few miles the weather was close to perfect. With a temperature of 50 degrees at most and overcast, only a swirling wind added difficulty to the race. Well run water stops and bands dotted the course as did visible mile markers and clocks every mile. I had, as I mentioned, designs on a PR.

214

Throughout this first half I encountered many people whom I had met at previous races and made lots of new friends as well. Christine made me a sign that said: "49 weeks 49 marathons" but it was apparently confusing to many who thought this was the end of my goal. I actually had to keep saying, "Well, I actually still have 3 more to go." Their incredulous response of "52? Wow!" made me laugh. When it had been 49 they were less than enthused. But 52, well that's a different story!

We soon entered the area for which the race is named, White Rock Lake. I noticed a power gel someone had dropped out of his back pocket right in front of me. Normally I might not have bothered but he looked back at it crestfallenly so I figured he really wanted it. So I scooped it up mid-run, sprinted ahead and told him that if he reached back like a relay runner I would hand it to him. Although I still saw two other gels in his shorts he treated this like a gift from the gods. He then looked back a few times directly at my bib number. I smiled and said, "I know, I know. 'Elite' my ass, right?" He smiled and said, "I just want to know who to thank when the race is over." I wonder if he felt the same at mile 23 when I passed him.

As the halfway point appeared I realized I had been really enjoying the run around the lake and was quite entertained by the herons flitting in and out of the water. I was a little slower than I wanted to be but felt refreshed. I knew the latter part of the course had some semi-tough uphills so I figured all I could do was give it my best.

The wind picked up in a few places around the lake but it was never really that much of a bother. Also, spectators began to show up to support the runners. Dallas is the fifth largest city in the country; a few more could not have hurt. However, unlike New York and other big city marathons, White Rock is not run strictly within the confines of the city. This obviously limits the opportunity for spectators to walk out of their house and cheer. Since I personally have never watched a marathon, who am I to complain?

Running out of White Rock Lake I came across a gentleman who I had run a few marathons with this year. He had run Marine Corps in October in a time of 3:05 (just behind me) for his 100th lifetime marathon. I was hoping to stay with him and chat but my energy was ebbing a little bit. I could tell that both the humidity from Cayman the week prior and the short turn-around to this race was not helping much. But I refused to crash and burn and I kept on chugging.

As we started a slight downhill that promised to continue for the last five miles, I picked up the speed. Suddenly, I caught a glimpse of a mass of humanity up ahead on the course and I could not figure out for the life of me what it was. As I drew closer I realized that this was where the half-marathoners were joining us. My pace was putting me smack dab into the biggest chunk of the half-marathons, all pushing for a 2-hour finish. To be honest, I was quite unhappy.

The halfers clogged the street with barely a smidgen of runner's etiquette among them, running five abreast at times. In spite of the many yelps from race volunteers that half runners must stay on the right to make way for passing marathoners, there was very little cooperation.

One runner shouted back, "We are running a race too!" I agree. I think the other racers deserve the same amenities that marathoners get but I think there should be different sections for each race distance. I do not think anyone would argue that full marathoners need more nourishment and assistance than those who have run considerably shorter distances. And besides, there should still be common courtesy. Marathoners have paid more to run and should not have to eat the leftovers of other runners. And do not get me started on non-runners eating food before runners get there or using race area porta-potties at the start. That's when all runners can unite in anger!

Nevertheless, to his endless credit, the race director found me after the race and asked for my honest opinions. He said he fully appreciated my candor in previous interviews and knew that catching me within minutes of my finish would allow him to find out even more about my true feelings without a filter.

I said, "Honestly, the only complaint I have is this last five miles."

He nodded immediately and said, "That will be fixed." He was happy to have the biggest field ever but unhappy that congestion had caused anyone to have a possible slower time. I knew he understood the enormity of the situation and I could already see the wheels turning. I had no doubt that the problem would be fixed for the next year.

Back to the race. As the crowd grew I began following a woman who had two pacers breaking the way through the crowd for her. I knew the gaps they were creating would quickly close, so I did my best to stay tight with them. A few surprise slight uphills sort of took some wind out of my sails but I was determined to get my new adjusted goal. Down to the last quarter mile or so, the crowds of spectators became more dense and the cheering started. As every person crossed the finish line, the announcer said his or her name and added a little commentary where he could. This would become even more difficult as the finishers crossed en masse, but I am pretty sure that he got every single runner.

"Let's welcome SuzyCaraSteveMarshallandAudrey as they finish the White Rock Marathon!"

I cruised in under 3:10 with a 3:09:36 for my fifth sub 3:10 in the last two months and my eighth fastest lifetime finish. I had reached my adjusted goal.

On the way home, I was swiftly reminded of my distaste for air travel. Sprinting through an airport mere hours after a marathon is not the recommended recovery, I do not think. Then after barely making the plane (I swear to god I threw my carry-on at a closing jetway door), we sat on the tarmac for over an hour before we finally took off.

Did I forget to mention the crying, nay, shrieking baby and the indifferent parents holding her?

One hundred fifteen flights down for the year. Just a few more to go.

46

The Final Three

Marathon 50
Race: Jacksonville Marathon, Jacksonville, FL
Miles from home: 708.5
1,310 miles raced
52.4 miles to race

Finishing Time: 3:10:20
Place: 51st

- I now have slightly more miles to run than I did last fall in my final tune-up race before Fiddy2: the JFK 50 mile race.
- Most people start their New Year's Eve countdown at 10 seconds. At the end of the marathon, it started for me at 1,222,022.

When I told someone recently that not only was I paying for the bulk of Fiddy2 myself but doing so without a credit card, the open-mouthed shock I received in return told me that racing over 1,300 miles this year was not nearly as impressive as not living on the plastic. It is responses like that and questions which were equally surprising ("What are you going to do with yourself in 2007?" was the most common one, as if I would wander around aimlessly bumping into objects in confusion) that kept things interesting

218

even as I was extremely excited to start a year where every weekend was not already planned.

As the year drew to an end, many would wish me luck and then laughingly say, "Ah, you do not need luck!" But I did. Every single day. The most current proof of this happened the weekend of this race.

Many months ago, I looked at the only two marathons on the continent for this weekend. One was in Washington state and the other was in Florida. But even if cheaper to fly to Washington, I would have picked Florida. And I would rather finish 51st amongst tough competition than third among weaker runners. Regardless, my luck prevailed again this year when not too long after finishing this race I heard that a snowstorm had called for the cancellation/postponement of the marathon.

The lesson? Luck matters. So does hard work and preparation. But I am getting ahead of myself. I still had this race to run.

In the starting area just a few minutes before the race, I saw a spectacularly nice woman named Helen, with whom I had run the better part of 20 miles all the way back in my third marathon of the year. She gave me a big hug and said she hoped she would run into me here. I met her husband who was running the half marathon and we all shared a few moments together as the race was slightly delayed. Soon, after Whitney Houston's Super Bowl XXV rendition of the Star Spangled Banner was played over the loud speakers, we were off.

One mile in, I knew what lay ahead. I was going to have to cover as much distance as quickly as possible because the temperature, cool at the start, was rapidly climbing. Humidity was going to be a major factor. How does a day with completely clear skies have a humidity of 98%?

Some who saw the sign on my back saying this was my 50th marathon of the year congratulated me and some said they had run with me a few weeks ago (when they actually ran with Dean Karnazes). We progressed through the miles. I joined with some people and either pulled away or fell back when I realized their pace was not my own. Today was going to be a day where I definitely had to run my own race.

The miles ticked away and I was actually feeling pretty good in spite of the humidity. As always, I hoped to run conservatively for the first half and turn it on for a negative split at the end. But then at mile 11, I ran an uncharacteristically slow mile for this part of the race. I am unsure if the mile was mis-marked or if I just had a slow mile but I erred on the side of caution and decided it was the latter. The next few miles were faster but I could see that the illusion of running comfortably beginning to fade. I decided to try and think about why people misuse apostrophes and quotation marks all the time, even on painted signs.

Uh-oh. While it would never come to this (I would drag my body across the finish first) my entire left leg began to beg me to stop. I would not have been startled by the pain if it had been confined to places that had been hurting for weeks. Unfortunately, with the quad twitching, the shin throbbing and the calf muscle screaming, I slowed down to ease the pain. I was far too close to the end to get injured.

Seriously, leg? You are still going to hurt like this?

Okay, I think it may be all right. Well not all right but back down to a manageable pain. Push on, wuss!

I still had a pretty darn good chance at running a 3:07 or 3:08. I just had to keep the pace I was now running. I did not think this would be a problem, as it appeared slowing down for the pain had saved me some extra energy. Furthermore, as much as the weather was warm and humid, the route was well shaded.

As I was trying to figure out my splits, an extremely toned woman passed me. I decided to try to run with her for motivation. She commented on the heat, and said I looked pretty good. I told her she was not too bad herself. Then I asked her if she was married (because flirting would help me get through the next four miles.) She laughed and flashed the compressed coal on her finger. I ended my flirtation.

We turned onto what I thought was the final straightaway. Unfortunately, the mossy tree-lined backstreets gave way to a highway with no shade, little charm and many cars. I had heard horror stories about blue-hairs damn near crushing runners to get to 9 am church but luckily none of that occurred around me on this day.

Our route took us to a stadium. I knew we would have to run a lap inside that stadium as well. I wanted to go sub 3:10 so bad that I could taste it. I entered the stadium and finally realized, there was too little time and too much track to go. A clock ahead showed me I was not going to make it.

However, running over a timing mat with around 250 yards to go, an announcer was given your name via computer and would announce it to the crowd. Of course, it would make more sense to me if it were closer so they could cheer as you finished but it was a nice touch indeed.

As I crossed the line, I held up one hand with all 5 digits spread and the other in the form of a Zero to let the photographers know that this was my 50th marathon for the year. I crossed in 3:10:18 and a friend from many races yelled out "Congrats on number 50 for the year, Dane!" which turned a few heads for sure. Drenched in sweat, I grabbed my medal and sat down on the nearest folding chair I could find. As a woman removed my timing chip, a chap came and asked for an interview. I asked him to give me a few seconds to grab a drink of water and then I would happily chat.

With sweat dripping down my face and salt in my mouth I answered some of the same questions I could pretty much recite in my sleep. Then the interviewer told me he had grown up near me.

"Really?" I said.

"Yeah, in Bayview."

I realized he thought I was from Titusville, Florida and not Titusville, Pennsylvania. I let him know I was from the Keystone State, downed a bottle of water and basked in the sun.

47

Make it Happen

Marathon 51
Race: Drake Well Marathon, Titusville, PA
Miles from home: Birthplace: 0; Present home: 333 miles
1,326.2 miles raced
26.2 miles to race

Finishing Time: 3:07:38
Place: 1st

One more marathon to go.

An uncomfortable possibility became a reality. Any chance of a marathon being run on the weekend before Christmas had officially moved from slim to none. For whatever reason, the so-called Christmas Marathon in Washington was to be run the week before Christmas. (Of course, the truth is that because of weather conditions the weekend before this, the race was postponed until December 23rd. However I'd had no idea that would occur.) I knew something needed to be done.

This year, I really think, could be called the year of the mutli-marathoner. Many runners, including myself, garnered press for running multiple marathons in 2006. With Dean Karnazes and Sam Thompson doing their 50 states in 50 days, Lance doing his New York marathon and many others doing feats to amaze, this was not quite the running boom of the late 1970s and early 1980s but a mini-boom indeed that threatened to spill over even further into the mainstream, I need not bore you with running statistics of the record number of marathon finishers in 2006 to prove my point.

As this year went on I became immersed not only in marathon running but in the history and traditions of marathons. Because of this and the hubbub surrounding marathons this year, I realized that I simply had to run a marathon on Christmas weekend that was a "real" marathon. Now, arguments can be made either way as to what makes a marathon "real". But I determined that one of the major details setting me apart from others this year was that I was running only certified marathons every single weekend in 2006, with no exceptions. I could not run a double on one weekend to make up for time where I was injured or because I wanted to take time off. I had turned down an offer to run the Tahoe Triple in Tahoe (which consisted of three marathons in three days.) While it would have afforded me some downtime later on in the year, it would not have been one marathon every weekend. Therefore, I had to run a race on either December 23rd or December 24th.

Most marathoners consider a marathon to be a timed race, run on the day it is advertised, with other competitors. At first I lent this theory little credence, as it appeared to be an elitist view. But it did not take many races until I was a convert. I figured, when I go home after work and run a 6.2-mile route, I should not consider myself the sole winner of the Dane Rauschenberg Start in my Back Yard 10k. Likewise, I could not possibly run a "fake" marathon on Christmas weekend and count it as a marathon towards Fiddy2. Therefore, my original idea of maybe running 26.2 miles on a treadmill or using a GPS to conjure a "marathon" distance went out the window. I had to either find a marathon or make one. And since I could not find one, it would be the latter.

But how could I possibly get a real course laid out with all the other things going on in my life? And where? Like a thunderclap the Drake Well Marathon was born, fittingly, while I was out on a run. I cannot exactly pinpoint when it hit me but it was so simple it was silly. I could put together a race in my hometown where the course layout was easy: run around a track until a marathon distance was covered. But that would not satisfy all the other requirements. So, I thought, get it certified, get other people to run it, make it chip-timed and the problem is solved.

Easier said than done of course. But when I get a hold an idea I refuse to let it go. (Case in point: my repeated failed attempts to get into the New York City Marathon. They only made me want to get into it more. While I did not resort to annoyances or backhanded deals, I did finally gain entry and was proud to run as part of the New York Fire Department's Haz Mat division). I had no idea, however, that the response to my seemingly odd idea would be so overwhelming.

I realized I was going to need help. I got in touch with my old high school track coach. As much as I despise delegating work, I lived six hours away from where the race was to take place, and knew I simply could not do this alone. Coach Henderson came through with flying colors. Before long, the track was secured. We got in touch with a man to do both the chip timing as well as the certification. Almost before I could blink, we were over the biggest hurdles.

Next, I enlisted my parents. My father, a skilled wood carver, was asked to make replicas of the historic Drake Well to act as a finisher's medal. Drake Well was the first fully-functioning drilled oil well in the world and it happens to be located in my hometown. The silhouette of the oil derrick is famous in the region and I thought it would make a fitting and unique medal. This was one of the many reasons I limited the race field to the first 25 runners, whoever they would be. The last thing I needed was to turn my Dad into a one-man sweatshop. When I got home the day before the race, the medals looked even better than I could have hoped them to be.

After that, I asked my mother to assist in assembling individualized runner's boxes to be given to each participant. Placed on a table on the track, the runners would have access to their boxes every quarter mile. My mother, not one to allow ugly boxes to litter the track, individually wrapped each box to look like a Christmas present and labeled all of the boxes with the names of the runners. In the boxes we placed each runner's choice of Gatorade, energy gels, water and homemade muffins. A table stocked with cold water on the far side of the track was provided to keep everyone hydrated.

Aunt Monica came through in the clutch. She arranged the services of a DJ who was instrumental in keeping us from all going insane, with a mixture of

Christmas music and tunes to keep the runners going. The Rock and Roll Marathons had nothing on my race.

The list could go on of all the wonderful ways that my family assisted me with this race but suffice it to say that without them I would never have been able to complete this marathon. I still get notes from the participants about the wonderful time they had.

My race could never have been completed without runners. I never thought that my limit of 25 runners would be reached so quickly but until the day before the race I was still turning runners away. Now this was especially hard to do as 100% of the registration fee to be donated to L'Arche Mobile, and every person I turned away was $100 less that I made for the charity. But beside the fact I did not want to overwork my father, I simply might be flirting with a colossal disaster trying to fit too many runners on a track at one time.

While due to injury or unforeseen circumstances, four runners did not make the trek to Titusville for the Inaugural Drake Well Marathon, the other 21 made it special indeed. As they are the reason this entire race was possible, I think I should tell you a little about each one of them.

Bib number 2: Larry Herman (Maryland)
Larry is a race director of the Frederick Marathon in Maryland and the very first person to sign up for the Drake Well Marathon. Back in July, at the San Francisco Marathon, we were having dinner with other runners when I told him about my idea for this race. Right then and there he signed up and said: "I want to be part of this." Bothered by an injury sustained during the JFK 50 mile race just a month prior, Larry gritted through tough ankle pain and made everyone smile with his wit. While he brought up the rear, never once did he grumble.

Bib number 3: David Terrill (Pennsylvania)
David and I met at the Hatfield & McCoy marathon in July. With a PR of 2:53, David was looking like he would be the winner of this race when the entrants came in. But having suffered his own injury as well just a few weeks before the race, he was slowed slightly. Regardless, he is one of the most stand up people you will ever meet. Truly kind and giving, we should all be so lucky to call people like Dave a friend. His third place overall was a thing a beauty. "I did not come here to start, I came here to finish." That should make your list

of quotes for 2008 and beyond.

Bib Number 4: Jim Roeder (Pennsylvania)
At 6'9", Jim was far and away the tallest competitor of the DWM. Jim is also an Ironman Triathlete, who set a 47-minute PR at the Drake Well Marathon! A fount of information on all things triathlon. To quote Jim:

"... thanks for the great day yesterday and the good fellowship at the pre-race meal Friday night...It was fun to have the run on the track as we were able to keep constant watch of our splits over a quarter of a mile. I think the surface was a little easier on the knees as well. All of the above factors helped me move my PR from 5:03:19 at the Marine Corp Marathon to 4:19:26 at the first annual Drake Well Marathon. I'll take it over Marine Corp and Disney any day."

Bib Number 7: Theresa Nosko Lyon (Virginia)
Ah, the Nosko girls. I say "girls" but I mean ladies in every sense of the word. These three sisters have been on the Fiddy2 bandwagon for quite some time and it was no surprise when they signed up to run the DWM. The overall woman's winner, Theresa did an awesome job on race day.

Bib Number 8: Julia Nosko Murray (Pennsylvania)
Julia told me that if we ever run the DWM again or if the course gets modified into more of a "real" race that she and her family would help in any way they could. Her friends and family accounted for a majority of the supporters and fans down at the track that Saturday morning.

Bib Number 9: Monica Copley (Pennsylvania)
In only her second marathon, with little to no training leading up to the race, Monica is a Titusville resident who said, "I can't rightfully pass up the opportunity to run a marathon one mile from my doorstep!"

Bib Number 11: Tracy Allen (Ohio)
I did not get to speak to Tracy as much as I would have wanted but after finishing the race I know he cared enough to send his family back down to the race to pick up his coveted Finisher's Medal!

Bib Number 13: Bonita Nosko Coats (Virginia)
Get this. For her first marathon ever, the third Nosko girl chose the DWM!

Color me flattered and impressed as I would never have taken on nearly 106 laps of a track as my first attempt at 26.2 miles! While her time was not a world-record, never once did she stop moving forward. True grit.

Bib Number 14: Damon Lease (Vermont)
Traveling all the way from Vermont, I know Damon was trying to qualify for Boston. Having already run well under 3 hours in his best time ever, I think a nagging injury got the best of him. Unfortunately he had to withdraw around mile 21. I did not get a chance to see him go before he left but wished him a speedy recovery later.

Bib Number 15: David Frame (Minnesota)
The birthday boy! Celebrating his 60th birthday, we welcomed David to Titusville before the race with a round of applause and serenaded him with the Beatles "Birthday Song" on the loud speaker. While he said the multiple loops got to him in the long run, David ran a race to be proud of. As a Minneapolis resident, he could appreciate how fortunate we were that for one of the only times in Titusville's history, there was no snow the day before Christmas.

Bib Number 16: Michael Yoder (Pennsylvania)
A quiet chap, Michael also set a personal best on the course by over 3 minutes (if I recall his words correctly.) Few things made my day more than hearing that not only did someone do well on this course described by some (who did not run it, by the way) as the worst thing they could imagine, but to set a personal best.

Bib Number 17: Annie Kirkland (Virginia)
Nearly a scratch before the race because of an injury, Annie and her lovely mother made the trip up from just a few miles away from me in Virginia. Annie is probably quite happy that she raced, as she took home 2nd place overall for the women! Way to go Annie!

Bib Number 18: Cowboy Jeff (Maryland)
What can I say about Jeff? Just an outstanding fella. Knowing I had too much on my plate, Jeff took it upon himself to organize the pasta dinner the night before the race. Conspiring with my mother (who made three kinds of dessert) to keep this a secret from me, Jeff made the dinner a success. A good number of the runners made it to the dinner. I cannot thank Jeff enough and am glad we met at the Little Rock Marathon all the way back in March. There

is a special place in heaven for folks like Jeff.

Bib Number 19: Eric Seremet (Colorado)
Eric put on such a strong showing that he was constantly spurring me to go faster. I am sure the air felt like heaven to his lungs as he is currently living in the high altitude of Colorado. Eric ended up taking second place overall for the entire race and we now have a 1-1 record against each other (he beat me in Estes Park earlier in the year).

Bib Number 20: Rick Parisi (Alabama)
I did not get to speak to Rick as much as I would like but I am glad he shed the warm winter fleece early in the race. He made me sweat every time I saw him. He and his lovely female friend, Gretchen, seemed quite pleased with his finishing time.

Bib Number 21: Melanie Dorland (Indiana)
Making the long drive from Indianapolis, Melanie, whose pretty face made many a runner stop and chat, had a very strong showing. With some of the most even split times on the day, Melanie chugged along like a machine. I hope she is very proud of her fourth place woman's finish, as I assuredly was.

Bib Number 22: Mary Siegel (Pennsylvania)
Bringing Hammer Gel for everyone, Mary was a welcome addition. Mary finished third overall for the women in style. With just a few steps to go, Mary turned around and backed over the finish line. Making quips all day, Mary was a joy to have on the track.

Bib Number 23: John O. Smith (Pennsylvania)
As the only one who left without removing his timing chip, he was the recipient of my first post-marathon email! Like many others he expressed that the race was wonderfully run and if there is a second version not only would he be there, but four members of his family would love to help.

Bib Number 24: Kelli Kleeb Staub (Pennsylvania)
The girls of this race were so generous. Kelli is a runner I met online earlier in the year, as well as in person at the Erie Marathon in September. She was one of the last people to sign up for the DWM but one of the ones I most enjoyed having at the race. Kelli brought Snickers Energy Bars for everyone and her

quick smile and cute little daughter made us all laugh. She scarcely looked tired as she finished the race and sat down to chat with her family.

Bib Number 25: Dan Geier (Pennsylvania)
With a large portion of his family in tow, Dan was quick with a smile and a joke. From his email after the race, Dan said:

"I enjoyed a PR yesterday...my Marine Corp was a 4:33.56...and my legs didn't bother me in D.C. like they did yesterday."

And noting how well my mother added surprises to the race, he talked about how the muffins and cake and cookies she had baked for the pasta dinner were so yummy."...with a mom like that, I'm surprised you don't weigh 250 lbs." He doesn't realize this is why I only go home twice a year. I would have to roll back afterwards.

Dan did not mention he had PR'd by 24 minutes!

That makes twenty-one starters, twenty finishers, at least four personal bests, nine states represented and with just a few snafus, I am pretty sure everyone had a wonderful time. With so much that could have gone wrong I think so much went perfectly.

And in a nice moment for myself, I was able to run a 3:07:38 and break the tape held by my aunt and mother to win a marathon for the first time ever.

Breaking the tape at the Drake Well Marathon was a great Christmas present.

48

Complete

Marathon 52
Race: Raced for the Ranch Marathon, Springfield, MO
Miles from home: 1088.5
1362.4 miles raced
0 miles to go

Finishing Time: 3:07:42
Place: 3rd

My research has shown that I am only the third person ever to run a marathon every single weekend in one calendar year. No one has done them faster.

So Fiddy2 came to a close. I had one last race to run. I would like to set both a personal best and set that personal best by a large margin. Did I have the energy left to do it? Would I be able to get out of the mindset of, "Oh, I have another one next week" and give it my all while reserving nothing? I was unsure. But I knew I would not fail from lack of trying. Yoda may have been right when he said: "Do or do not. There is no try." You do indeed either do something or you do not. Then again, Yoda never ran a marathon. He was also a puppet.

Anyone who told me that the eight plus laps of this 5k course would be monotonous obviously knew very little about Fiddy2. Having done almost every conceivable course design during the year, including last week's 106 laps of a track (which, much to my surprise was far more enjoyable than I could have ever hoped), eight measly laps were going to be a cakewalk. That is, of course, if those 3 miles were enjoyable to begin with. If, for example, the course had a monster hill, repeated running of it would be far from my cup of tea.

So, for one of the few times his year, I decided to scope out the course beforehand. My friend Jenny joined me as she had come to run the race as well. Even though we left virtually the same time from the same airport, we took different routes and landed at different times.

As we drove the course we realized it was not just eight laps of a circle. Rather it was eight laps, with a few uphills and tons of turns where you would be able to see other runners. We wondered on which lap those hills would stop looking like molehills and erupt as mountains.

We grabbed some pasta the night before the race and went back to the hotel and settled in. With the 3pm start, we were unsure of when to fall asleep, when to get up, when to eat and what to eat. So we climbed into our beds and decided to wake up when we woke up. The next day started with interviews with a local paper as well as a television affiliate and I recounted my story for probably the 10,000th time this year. I never tire of telling it. I am sure my friends get tired of hearing it!

Much to our chagrin, the forecasted 40-50s temperature ended up being 10 degrees cooler. Gusting winds whipped around Springfield, making it even chillier. Jenny and I debated long sleeves, pants, hats and gloves.

In the gym of a local church I ran into some old friends, made some new friends and was flattered often. One gentleman was running his first marathon ever and drove all the way from Kansas City.

He said, "I wanted to run a race with you."

I realized if I was going to try and calculate my pace I was probably going to need a slide rule. With no visible mile markers, we would simply have to take the first lap around (4.5 miles) and add the 5k every lap and then extrapolate. At least I would have math to keep me busy.

As we made the loops I could not decide how I felt. Internally, I felt like I was pushing it and with only two marathoners in front of me, I felt my pace was good. Moreover, a fellow runner with whom I had run several times this year (and who had beaten me in every race but the Marine Corps Marathon) was right on my heels, so I knew I was not going too slow. And damn it Brad, I could not shake you!

So the 13.8-mile marker hit and I thought I was well under the pace to run a sub-3 hour marathon. Then I did more math and realized what I thought was a 1:29 was actually a 1:34.

Still unable to shake Brad, I figured he would be passing me at any point. He had been inching closer every lap and we had exchanged salutations every time. I love the fact that in running you can be so competitive and so friendly at the same time. I have run many races this year with people I would be racing to the wire with but with whom I was not going to be angry if they bested me. And if I ever found the other was holding back for any reason I would be livid!

We passed the turn-around to begin the last two laps. Darkness had set in and the volunteers were absent. Only one or two hearty souls manned the water station at one turn-around point in a parking lot. (I do not entirely blame them. The wind and rain were bitterly cold.) On my first trip through this lot I had slipped on the wet pavement rounding a cone and did a split. Sure did loosen the groin. Someone must have seen me as the cone was moved five feet to the right the next time through. That was greatly appreciated.

Brad had fallen back a step. With first and second place runners solidly in front of me, it was now a battle for third. My legs were hurting but I figured if I had anything left in them I might as well use it here. There were no more races to run in 2006. All I had to do was go up one hill, make a left turn, go down a straightaway, make another turn and back up another hill. Every other lap, I had been able to see Brad as I made one of those last turns. This time, I could not see him. This scared me and made me press even harder.

Up the straightest, steepest portion of the course, I knew I had about 1.5 miles to go. Around the slippery cone, I grabbed my last Powerade from the lone volunteer who remained and saw Brad was further behind than usual. As we slapped hands again, he said, "She's all yours. Go get her." I decided to leave nothing to chance. Down the hill, make a right, around the park for the eighth time and the church and finish line were in sight.

One last look behind me showed a clear street. No one was going to sneak in behind me. I crossed the finish line in 3:07:42, four seconds slower than last week but my sixth fastest time of the year. A volunteer tore the tag from my bib number and I quickly ran to my car. My shirts were drenched with sweat and rain and were beginning to ice. I tore off the wet shirts, threw my race t-shirt on, grabbed my fleece jacket and cell phone. Checking messages, I strolled to the church area and into the basketball court where people were warming themselves. I was met by a reporter walking out to watch me finish. I told her, with a laugh that she was too late. She began to ask me a few questions and I told her she'd have to wait. My parents needed to know I was finished.

After I spoke to my mom and a select few friends, it finally hit me: I was done. It must have been a little dusty in the back room of the rec area of the church, because my eyes seemed to be watering.

I answered the reporter's questions, said hello to some friends, ate a bowl or two of chili and ran back outside. An incoming call from BBC radio was being routed to my hotel room, and the original plan had been to field the call and head back out to pick up Jenny who expected to finish about an hour behind me. Well, as nice as the BBC is, I decided they too would have to wait. Running back onto the course, I found Jenny about half a mile from the finish. Midway through the race, when we crossed paths, I had told her I had changed plans and would wait for her. When she saw me, she smiled as much as her frozen lips would allow and we headed towards the finish together. To her credit she left me in the dust, so I cut across a field to cheer her on at the finish. As she crossed the line, less than an hour after I had, she barely looked winded.

We hopped into the car and drove back to the hotel. Jenny thawed out in the shower and my phone rang. After confirming with the reporters in

London that 2007 had arrived there, I exchanged pleasantries with the Brit folks about Fiddy2.

After the call, I grabbed a shower and we rushed back to the gym. I hoped to say hello to some more friends but the gym was almost empty. So we feasted on the warm food and said a whole bunch of nothing. Jenny found out she was sixth overall (women) and received a nice little boot trophy (it was the Run for the Ranch Marathon) for her efforts. At last we headed back to the hotel, to settle down and watch the ball drop. I had never experienced New Year's Eve in any time zone other than the East Coast.

Soon after "our" midnight, our beds called. I lay there for a very short time before I fell asleep. I have never had trouble in that respect. But before I dropped off I am pretty sure I smiled.

I was done.

Finishing in the dark, in 3rd place overall, Dane completes his 52nd marathon of the year at the Run For the Ranch Marathon on New Year's Eve.

49

Going Home

My last flight of the year is delayed? Are you kidding me?

My flight was lacking pilots (how in the name of all that is good and holy does a plane not have a frickin pilot?) leaving me with the option of two different flights. One would get me in around 2am. The other would be to fly into Philadelphia and make the drive home. I opted for the latter, only because Anne mentioned she would pick me up.

So after a later flight to Chicago, then a flight to Philly, then a two-plus hour drive back to DC (all of which made me miss Penn State's New Year's Day bowl game), I spent the first day of 2007 remembering what made all of 2006 so difficult.

I definitely was not going to miss any of this.

50

Acquiescence

I sat on my couch a few days after the Springfield Marathon and thought.

For the first time in almost two years I approached a weekend where I did not need to do a single thing. No flight to catch. No reason to carb load. No marathon to run. Wait. No marathon to run? Ever since the idea hit me to run 52 consecutive weekly marathons in one calendar year in March of 2005, I had been planning. Air travel. Hotels. Rental cars. Looking at weather maps in places I normally would not even know existed. I knew why people asked me if I knew what to do with myself in 2007. I had been ensconced in a weekly routine for the better part of 22 months and it was now done. Just like that.

I felt a sense of relief. Being a confident person I never would have undertaken Fiddy2 if I had not felt it was possible. I am surprised, however, with just about every other aspect about it. Those who supported me. Those who did not. How the most tiring and exhausting part was not the marathons but the constant travel and the endless fundraising. I have forever had my viewpoint changed of those who work to raise money for causes that mean a great deal to them. There is never a rest period.

Disappointments will be forgotten, as successes will become amplified. The enormity of this accomplishment will possibly hit me as I become distanced from the year. As it stands, I remain generally unimpressed. This is not false modesty. This is just me. I generally feel that if I can accomplish something, many other people might be able to do so as well.

There are many things in this world we cannot do. Trying is not one of them. Chances are someone has said that before and with far more eloquence than I. I do not believe that we can do anything if we try. That, to me, is a wonderfully sunny view of the world, which I do not subscribe to. We do have limits. We all have hurdles, which, for one reason or another, we will never be able to get over. I have absolutely no problem with that. What I do have a problem with is accepting those absolutes and allowing them to deter us from, at the very least, attempting to achieve. As I said, humans are blessed with selective memory and a sense of distorted reality when it comes to what they can achieve.

A new year and a new life lay before me. What would I do with them? I wasn't quite sure. But I did know that succeed or fail, I would go down fighting.

I know no other way to live.

51

Fiddy2 Stats

Miles flown: Over 80,000
Time zone changes: 56
States: 26 (and D.C.)
Countries: 3 (Cayman, Canada and the US)
Provinces: 2
Days slept in my own bed: 243

Marathons over 4 hours: 1 (Leadville)

Marathons over 3:30: (Excluding Leadville) 6
01.08.06 Walt Disney World Marathon FL 3:48:18
01.21.06 Gold's Gym Orlando Xtreme Marathon FL 3:40:06
01.29.06 ING Miami Tropical Marathon FL 3:31:30
02.19.06 Washington's B-Day Marathon MD 3:30:59
04.15.06 Charlottesville Marathon VA 3:31:55
06.18.06 Estes Park Marathon CO 3:36:23

Marathons under 3:20: 31 in total

Boston Qualifiers for male 30 years of age: 11
(all occurred in the last 3.5 months of 2006)

09.10.06 Erie Marathon at Presque Isle PA 3:10:17
10.01.06 Johnstown Marathon PA 3:05:10
10.15.06 Des Moines Marathon IA 3:10:12
10.21.06 Niagara Falls Marathon NY/ON 2:59:48
10.29.06 Marine Corps Marathon VA 3:03:54
11.05.06 New York Marathon NY 3:05:43
11.25.06 North Central Railway Trail Marathon MD 3:09:54
12.10.06 Dallas White Rock TX 3:09:36
12.17.06 Jacksonville Marathon FL 3:10:20
12.24.06 Drake Well Marathon PA 3:07:38
12.31.06 Run for the Ranch Marathon MO 3:07:42

***Three of the four fastest marathons of my life
(at the end of 2006)
were run in a 3 week span from 10.22.06 - 11.05.06**

***Six of Ten of the fastest Marathons ran in my life
(at the end of 2006)
were done this year.**

52

Most Asked
Questions

Q: How far is a Marathon?

A: Always too long. Or 26.2 miles.

Q: Why 52 Marathons?

A: The idea evolved from the fact that running a marathon in every state was not nearly the novel idea I thought it was at first. (Hundreds of people have accomplished the feat). So I took it up a notch.

Q: Why L'Arche Mobile?

A: What started as chance proved to be fate when I, searching for marathons in 2006, came upon the Legg Mason First Light Marathon in Mobile, Alabama that benefited L'Arche Mobile. It took me no time to realize this was an organization that needed to be the beneficiary of Fiddy2.

Q: How will my Donation Help L'Arche?

A: All funds raised will be used for unrestricted operating expenses, special projects, building improvements and endowments.

Q: Is my Donation Tax Exempt?

A: L'Arche Mobile is a charitable organization and is tax-exempt under 501 (c)(3) by the IRS. Therefore, donations made to L'Arche Mobile are tax-deductible.

Q: Is this healthy?

A: I would never attempt anything that I feel would permanently jeopardize my health. I like myself far too much for that. However, I most assuredly do not think that what I am doing is for everyone but I do know that we never know what we can do until we find out what we cannot. And presently, I know I can run a great deal with little rest.

Q: Is this your job?

A: No. I still have an occupation where I put in over 50 hours a week during the regular workweek.

Q: Did you have an airline sponsor?

A: Presently I have no sponsorships with any airline to help defray costs of Fiddy2.

Q: Who pays for your hotels?

A: The guy answering these questions. (i.e. me)

Q: Why not just give the money you spend on travel and marathons directly to L'Arche?

A: This is a multiple answer. First, I am new at fundraising. In my naivety, I assumed that corporations wishing to help would cover a majority of my costs. As for individuals, I know we often need more than just the knowledge that "it is for a good cause" to give up our hard-earned money. So, by doing something few, if any, have ever done, I thought I was giving enough of myself to make others desire to open their checkbook.

Second, I could have never expected the costs of flying would be as high as they are (due to ongoing wars, Hurricane Katrina and other hurricanes, etc.)

Third, even if large amounts of money from many good-willed people do not pour in as I near the end, I have at least raised awareness of L'Arche and its mission.

And finally, the idea of Fiddy2 came about before I even decided to raise money "on the side", so to speak. The wheels were in motion to take on this task before my affiliation with L'Arche began.

Q: How do you choose which marathons you run?

A: Many factors go into choosing the marathons I run. As I am footing the bill for this excursion, it usually boils down to a matter of which marathon costs the less or will allow me to return to my job. However, some are chosen for sentimental reasons or because of relationships I have developed with other runners.

Q: What shoes do you wear?

A: I do not have a single brand or type that I prefer. In fact, once I had to wear a pair of shoes purchased the night before the race as I had forgotten my shoes at home. I ran my fastest marathon of the year up to that point that day.

Q: Can you eat anything you want?

A: Unfortunately, I cannot. In fact, as I am not running as many miles during the week as I normally would, I actually have to watch what I eat to some extent.

Q: How much do you run during the week?

A: I usually only have time to get about 3 runs in during the week for a total of 10-15 miles. Fundraising and working does not allow for much time to train. My "training" was last year (2005) when I pushed my body to see if it could hold up to the rigors of multiple long-distance races.

Q: Are you trying to run a marathon in every state this year?

A: Given the nature of my task to run one every single weekend, it is virtually impossible to reach every state in 2006.

Q: How much do you weigh?

A: Approximately 180 lbs.

Q: Do you have a family?

A: I am currently single.

Q: Are you tired?

A: Quite. Thank you for asking.

Q: Have you suffered any injuries or have you been ill?

A: Yes to both but nothing that has stopped me.

244

Q: How do you stay mostly injury free?

A: We give advice based on our experience and what we do to get there. Based on my experience you stay injury free by running 52 marathons in a year! More seriously, I train hard, have luck on my side and was smart enough to pick the right parents.

Q: Will you be able to successfully complete Fiddy2?

A: The surest way to guarantee failure is to never try. That said, I have complete faith that I will accomplish this goal. Besides the drive and the heart to succeed, I also have put in the time and the training needed to see this goal through to the end of 2006. I will be happy to take all bets against me.

Q: What will you do next year?

A: Nap. A lot.

Q: Do you take your shorts off all the way to pee?

A: What?

Q: Are you going to do all 52 states?

A: *Silence* *Dane walks away*

MORE TITLES
from The Experience Publishers

The Experience Publishers